THE NAVIGATORS
LED OR MISLED

JERRY WELTER

authorHOUSE®

AuthorHouse™
1663 Liberty Drive
Bloomington, IN 47403
www.authorhouse.com
Phone: 833-262-8899

This book is a work of non-fiction. Unless otherwise noted, the author and the publisher make no explicit guarantees as to the accuracy of the information contained in this book and in some cases, names of people and places have been altered to protect their privacy.

Published by AuthorHouse 04/18/2022

ISBN: 978-1-6655-5693-4 (sc)
ISBN: 978-1-6655-5694-1 (e)

Library of Congress Control Number: 2022907226

Print information available on the last page.

This book is printed on acid-free paper.

Contents

Acknowledgements

To my Lord and Savior Jesus Christ, who gave me the revelation for this message; words are not enough to describe all of the blessings you have given me, and the things you have done in my life. I'm eternally grateful! I can only pray for the grace to continue to share the timeless truth of the Gospel.

To my amazing wife, Yolande, who has stood unwaveringly by my side for the past 22 years and has always believed the best in me. I love you!

To my mother, Cheryl Smiley, who taught me the gospel and never gave up praying for me; I love you mom! To Matt Smiley, you have stepped into my life and became the Father my dad never had the chance to be. I love you Matt.

To my son Brandon, who is always reminding me how creation declares the glory of God. I'm blessed to have you as my son. To my daughter, Jessi, who never gives up, and challenges me to keep my eyes on the Lord. I'm so proud of you.

I want to thank John Bevere and Messenger International for giving permission to share quotes. John and Lisa, your ministry has shaped, changed, and challenged the lives of my family and me. My wife and I are *eternally* grateful!

I also want to thank Jay Vincent for his encouragement and mentoring during this project. Also, a big thank you to Eric George, Jim Lee, and Rich & Connie Taylor, for their feedback and encouragement.

I would also like to thank Frank Baldwin, and the Muncie Mission Ministries, for the opportunity to serve on the front lines for the kingdom! To all my friends at MMM, keep fighting "the good fight."

I need to give a special thanks to Buddy Dow for his publishing expertise and mentoring through this process.

To all my family and friends who were involved in this project, I don't have room to name everyone individually – but thank you! I've been so blessed by all your encouragement! I thank you, and may God richly bless all of you for your support!

Choice One

The Waters of Destiny

I should tell you this is not a book on politics. I say that because I know the *red* and *blue* on the cover could lead your mind to political parties (there *is* a meaning behind the colors, but more on that later). Neither is this a book on conspiracy theories or self-help. This is more than a book — this is a guide to help you navigate through the waters of life, so you can reach the shores of your destiny.

Before we had GPS devices, sailors would use the lights in the sky to navigate their way across the seas. Whether you are a leader, or a follower, or somewhere in between, we all have something that we are following as we go through life. You may be following a dream, a vision, a goal, a relationship or some other "thing." No matter what it is, we all have something that we are following as a guide for our lives. The question is: "are the lights we are following guiding us *closer* to the plans and purposes God has for our lives, or farther *away*?"

God has a plan, purpose, and destiny for your life. We often realize all too late that the lights we are following are actually misleading us — taking us farther away from God's best plan for our lives. We have to learn how to discern among the lights to navigate through the waters of life and find our way to the purposes and plans God has for our lives. There are so many lights out there that seem to be shining the way to destiny, but in actuality they are leading us in the opposite direction of what God has for us. Reaching God's destiny for our lives hinges on the choices we make. In this guide, there are no chapters — only choices. The choices we make in life will determine whether we are being led to our destiny or misled to our destruction.

God says:

> I call heaven and earth to witness against you today that I have set before you life and death, the blessing and the curse. *Therefore, choose life*, that you may live, you and your descendants. (Deuteronomy 30:19, WEB)

We all face life and death choices every day. Every choice either moves us closer to, or farther away, from what God has for us. Now, I want to encourage you that, no matter where you are in life, whether you have missed opportunities, made intentional or accidental mistakes, or are searching to find your way back, after being lost; your past, your race, your gender, your background, your financial status, your marital status — *none* of it limits God and His plans for your life.

"I know what I'm doing. I have it all planned out—
plans to take care of you, not abandon you, plans
to give you the future you hope for." (Jeremiah
29:11, MSG)

God not only has a plan and a purpose for your future,
but He also specializes in using all things, (i.e., the good, the
bad, and even the ugly) to work together to bring you into your
destiny. The apostle Paul assures us of this:

"We know that all things work together for good
for those who love God, for those who are called
according to his purpose." (Romans 8:28, WEB)

I love how Paul says, "all things." God is so infinite and able
that He says, "All things." He is telling us to "fill in the blank"
and He will work it all out! God wants you going in the right
direction toward what He has for your life! In fact, He had plans
for you before you were born. Before you ever did anything
right or wrong, he chose YOU!

"Before I formed you in the womb, I knew you.
Before you were born, I sanctified you." (Jeremiah
1:5, WEB)

The word "sanctified" means "set apart." God set you apart
for a purpose *before* you were born! So, if you are reading this,
He has *not* rejected you! He has *chosen* you! He has chosen
you to be an instrument of His redemptive grace and power;
He has a place and a platform for you, and a calling for you to
fulfill. However, in knowing and believing this, you also have

to know that you have an enemy who also has a plan — for your destruction. He seeks to lead you astray from the plans and purposes that God has for you. The apostle Peter wrote, "Be sober and self-controlled. Be watchful. Your adversary, the devil, walks around like a roaring lion, seeking whom he may devour" (1 Peter 5:8, WEB). The Devil does not want you to reach your destination in life. He has always been looking for ways to mislead God's people.

As I was preparing this guide, and praying for wisdom, I was reminded of an experience I had on a beach years ago. I did not realize at that time the magnitude of what I was seeing and how God would use my experience to create what you now have in front of you. I have heard it said, if you want to hear God laugh tell him your plans, but I think it's also true the other way around. I think when God tells us His plans, we laugh! I never would have imagined that God would give me a message using a phenomenon of nature as a revelation to lead people to the waters of their destiny, and to explain complex things from His word, and yet here we are and here is how it happened.

A few years ago, I was on one of the beaches in Gulf Shores, Alabama. It was in the month of June, and I remember walking along the beach, looking out to a seemingly endless sea. The sun was shining, and the white caps were riding the waves. I could listen to the sound of those waves for hours. While I was walking, I noticed dozens of places (not far from the shoreline), where little plastic nets formed a square about a foot high. They were not big areas; they only marked off a few square feet. I decided to do some research — I inquired of some of the locals and found out that those areas were marked off to protect sea turtle nests that were buried beneath the sand. There are people that monitor the beach for sea turtles and their nests to protect the hatchlings once they emerge.

One night, I just happened to be on the beach when I saw a young woman by the nest; she was there monitoring the nest because the sea turtles were about to hatch. Now, where I'm from, a landlocked state in the Midwest, this is a rare opportunity. I began asking her questions about the process, and she said she has to be here to help the hatchlings make it to the ocean. She went on to say that the turtles are led to the sea by following the moonlight. However, because of all the artificial lighting from the condominiums, cars, and parking lots that the majority of the hatchlings are easily misled by the other lights. As a result, many are run over by cars, eaten by predators, or die of dehydration because they never make it to the sea.

That night, I waited for hours for those hatchlings to emerge, and finally the waiting paid off. They came popping out of the sand just as the lady had said. They began going in all directions because they were so disoriented by all the other lights. I personally just wanted to pick them up and carry them to the water, but you're not supposed to touch them; they have to make it to the ocean on their own. There was a way to intervene without physically relocating them, and my new friend came prepared. She brought a flashlight that shone red; she would shine the light on the ground in front of the tiny turtles and they would follow her red light to the sea. It was fascinating to watch them pierce the sand and follow her light as they persevered toward the water. As I was reflecting in that moment, God began to give me the revelation of how He leads us to our destiny. I could see how God shines His light for us to follow, just like this woman was helping the turtles, and I remembered the words of Jesus in John's gospel. Jesus spoke to them, saying, 'I am the light of the world. He who follows me will not walk in darkness but will have the light of life' (John 8:12, WEB).

God is definitely shining a light for us to follow. But again, you and I face the same danger as those hatchlings, and it's those artificial lights out there that the Devil shines to mislead us. In fact, the Bible says, "And no wonder, for even Satan masquerades as an angel of light" (2 Corinthians 11:14, WEB). This is where you need to use caution; if you don't know how to distinguish the true light from the artificial lights, you could easily miss the way. Only one light leads to life, while the other lights lead to death. Just as there was someone to guide those hatchlings to the sea, it is my hope that this guide will illuminate the one light that will lead you to the waters of your destiny — God's best for your life.

Now, something else came to my mind as I thought about those little sea turtles. As big as their target (the ocean) is, if they don't make it to the water, they are easy prey. As I said earlier, they may get snatched up by a predator, or die somewhere in an arid place. And here's the thing: none of the predators that threaten them are very big when compared to the size of the many creatures and predators in the ocean — yet those turtles can survive out at sea for over a hundred years! I realized the reason they are such easy prey is because they are out of their environment. I know that may sound simple, but it's really profound if you think about it.

You see, they were created for something bigger! Once those little ones, so helpless on the sand, hit the ocean, they were unstoppable. It was amazing how fast they could go! It's as if they were transformed into something supernatural the minute they hit the water. That's when it hit me! It's the same for you — if you don't make it to the waters of your destiny and find the life you were created to live by fulfilling your purpose, then you are out of your environment, and you too will die. You may not die instantly, but you will begin to die slowly on the inside. At best you will find yourself existing, going through the motions. You cannot survive, let alone thrive, apart from your destiny. Out of the billions of people who have walked the earth, there has never been anyone just like you. You are unique — an original — and only you can do what God created you to do. You will never be truly fulfilled until you find the life only you can live.

Another thing we can learn from these little hatchlings is trust. They are subatomic in comparison with the vastness of the ocean, and yet they fearlessly swim out to meet the water they were destined to join. Just like those sea turtles, you were created for something so much bigger. You are subatomic compared to your destiny; it's bigger than you could even imagine. The life you were meant to live is just in front of you, and once you find it, something supernatural will happen to you too. You have to allow yourself to respond; feel the ocean breeze, smell the salty air, and see the sun coming up on the horizon. Imagine yourself saturated in the promise, presence, provision, and power of God. The turtles have given us a beautiful example of how to follow the light that leads to the waters of destiny. The life God has predestined for you to live is the destination. God has plans for your life that you have never thought of; that have never entered into your mind.

"Before we were even born, he gave us our destiny; that we would fulfill the plan of God who always accomplishes every purpose and plan in his heart." (Ephesians 1:11, TPT)

And in this passage, He reminds us He is more than able to do it!

"Now to him who is able to do immeasurably more than all we ask or imagine, according to his power that is at work within us, to him be glory in the church and in Christ Jesus throughout all generations, for ever and ever!" (Ephesians 3:20, NIV)

This verse from Ephesians confirms it. God's plans for your life go beyond your imagination! If you can imagine what God has in store for you – it's not God! He goes beyond the capacity of your imagination! It is time for you to make your first choice (remember, this is a guide not a book). I cannot choose for you which light to follow, in the same way I could not carry those little ones to the sea. No one can make this choice for you; this is actually for your benefit. A word of advice from experience: *Do not skip around!* If you do, you could just as easily be misled. Do the hard work of going through, choice by choice, seeking the waters of your destiny — God's best for you! No matter where you are in this moment in your life, it is not too late for you! All you have to do in this choice is *believe!*

"For He says, 'In the time of my favor I heard you, and in the day of salvation I helped you.' I tell you, now is the time of God's favor, now is the day of salvation." (2 Corinthians 6:2, WEB)

CHARTER GUIDE ONE
"The Waters of Destiny"

Charter Guide

A charter is something you rent to transport you by air, land, or sea. Once you make a choice; that is going to be the vehicle (i.e., charter) that either takes you closer to your destiny, or farther away. At the end of every choice (i.e., chapter), is a charter guide with questions for your reflection.

Your first choice is to *believe*:

- What is your understanding of God's purpose for your life?

- Does knowing God has a plan, a purpose, and a destiny for you to fulfill encourage you to seek Him and His plans for your life?

- What changes need to happen in your heart in order to re-route from your own plans to God's bigger plans for your life?

- How can you allow God to make the most of your story, even if you've just come to know Him?

- What from your past threatens your ability to believe that you can now access God's best for your life in the future?

THE CHOICE

This is your first choice, you have to *choose to believe,* to believe that God has a good plan and a purpose for your life and a destiny for you to fulfill, or you can choose *not to believe,* the choice is yours to make.

Scripture: "Before we were even born, he gave us our destiny; that we would fulfill the plan of God who always accomplishes every purpose and plan in his heart." (Ephesians 1:11, TPT)

Thought: You cannot survive, let alone thrive, apart from your destiny. Out of the billions of people who have walked the earth, there has never been anyone just like you. You are unique — an original — and only you can do what God created you to do. You will never be truly fulfilled until you find the life only you can live.

NOTES:

Choice Two

The Light *of* the World, or the Lights *in* the World

When I think about how those hatchlings scattered in every direction once they emerged, following the first light they saw; it reminded me of this verse:

"There is a way which seems right to a man, but in the end it leads to death." (Proverbs 14:12, WEB)

Have you ever felt so certain about a decision, or a relationship, or a job, only to discover things did not work out at all the way you thought they would? It seemed right, it felt right, everyone was on board with you; people were even encouraging you! But, in the end, you watched everything go up in flames! It's the same for those little hatchlings; they think they are going in the right direction. They don't understand that without the help of someone shining the red light to lead them away from all the artificial lights, that they each have very little chance of finding the right path alone. In fact, the odds are that only 1 percent will make it to the ocean without someone there to guide them.

It's the same for us! If we don't have a light to guide us, we are heading for destruction. The lies of the enemy are so deceiving that the only way to discern the true light from among the artificial lights of the Devil is to *know the truth.* King David said:

> "Truth's shining light guides me in my choices
> and decisions; the revelation of your Word makes
> my pathway clear." (Psalm 119:105, TPT)

The truth is found in the Word of God; it is the Light that guides us as we navigate our way through this life.

The Guiding Light

I learned something several years ago that totally changed the way I view truth. I was leading a recovery group for men and women who were struggling with various addictions, hurts, habits, and hang ups — people just trying to find their way. We were studying the definition of insanity. Now, insanity is defined as "doing the same thing over and over and expecting a different result." And *that is crazy!* However, I wanted to go a little deeper, because I felt there was more to insanity than just repeating yourself. So, I looked up the definition of *sanity,* because sometimes looking at the opposite of something gives you a clearer picture of the actual meaning of both things. As

I researched the definition of sanity, I learned *sanity* is best defined as, "the ability to make a decision based on truth."

By that definition, *insanity* could be better defined as, "the *inability* to make a decision based on truth."

Here is what totally transformed the way I view truth. I realized that in order to distinguish the difference between someone who is sane and someone who is insane (by way of reason), that there must be a *standard* for truth that we can all reference. This objective truth has to be the standard for all of us when determining if the thoughts, ideas, and all of the distracting "lights" in the world that bombard us are leading us to make decisions that are *sane* (based on the truth) or *insane* (not based on the truth).

Jesus said the word of God is the truth, (John 17:17). Jesus came to give us a reference for truth so that we would not be misled by the lies Satan disguises as truth. How interesting that, just as those hatchlings followed a red *light*, we follow the red *letters*. In most bibles, the words of Jesus are printed in **red**! Now, just to be clear, the *whole* bible contains the words of Jesus, even when He is not being directly quoted. John testifies to this, "*The Word* became flesh, and lived among us. We saw his glory, such glory as of the one and only Son of the Father, full of *grace* and *truth*" (John 1:14, WEB).

We are to compare all our own thoughts and ideas, and the suggestions the world throws at us, against the "***red light***" of His word. His word is the light of truth that guides us along the way; we have to choose to follow *His* light. If His word is not the final authority for our lives, we will be deceived by the lights of the Devil. Here is a sobering thought: *your destiny hinges on what you choose to believe is truth*! Jesus said:

> I have come as a light into the world, that whoever believes in me may not remain in the darkness. If anyone listens to my sayings, and doesn't believe, I don't judge him. For I came not to judge the world, but to save the world. He who rejects me, and doesn't receive my sayings, has one who judges him. The word that I spoke will judge him in the last day. (John 12:46 - 48, WEB)

Here is an example of what Jesus is saying: let's say you are with someone who doesn't believe in gravity, and you're both standing on the edge of a cliff, two-hundred feet above sea level, enjoying a panoramic view, when your friend says he is going to jump down for a closer look! Because he is your friend, you try to persuade him — telling him that he will fall to his death if he jumps! You were not condemning your friend for his unbelief; you were trying to save him with your words — with the truth! If he still jumps, gravity will be the judge, not you. It is a sobering passage, because it tells of coming judgment, but at the same time, it is encouraging. Jesus became a man, to be a light to the Earth, to show us the truth! Jesus explained this to Pilate, "For this reason I have been born, and *for this reason* I have come into the world that I should testify to the truth. Everyone who is of the truth listens to my voice" (John 18:37, WEB).

Today, truth is an endangered species. More and more we are being told by the world that truth is whatever the individual believes to be true. The Apostle Paul warned us that the time would come when truth would not be tolerated:

For the time will come when *they will not listen* to the sound doctrine, but having itching ears, will heap up for themselves teachers after their own lusts, and will turn away their ears from the truth, and turn away to fables. (2 Timothy 4:3-4, WEB)

The light of Jesus reveals the true nature and character of God — truth in its most perfect form. We follow His light by studying His word, teachings, and way of life. Following His light is what enables us to see through the lies of the enemy. He came as a light to illuminate the way of truth for us. I believe, and I *know*, that the word of God is *the* Truth, with a capital T. Remember insanity is that which results from not having a standard of truth to guide our decisions. Here is an example of the insanity we see today:

Imagine you're building a house. You have all the materials, labor, and resources you need for the project. However, through a crazy chain of events, the blueprint for the house has been lost! In case you're not familiar with blueprints, a blueprint has pages and pages of pictures and drawings of the design of the house. It shows how to build the foundation, where the rooms are to be built, where the wiring and plumbing is located; it is the true picture of what the house is supposed to look like when it is whole from the inside out. Imagine what would happen if you told your crews to start building the house without the blueprint! They would have no standard, no guide! The crews would be arguing over the design of the house, where the bathrooms go, how big the rooms should be, how deep the foundation goes, what the pitch of the roof should be, will it be an open concept or not — it would be total chaos! This is what it is like when you lack a standard of truth in your life. It's chaos. It's *insanity.*

Without a reference for truth, the world falls into chaos. *–Jerry Welter*

With this thought in mind, let's look at how comparing the light of the truth of God's word against the artificial lights Satan disguises as truth, and how it gives us a clearer picture of the truth as God would have us see it.

Discerning Among the Lights

Light reveals everything that the darkness tries to hide. I did some research on the color spectrum of light and discovered that **blue** is the dominant color in both natural light and artificial light. No wonder those hatchlings struggle to find the true light — they are all disguised as natural light! To see the big picture of the truth we need the right filter. We don't hear a lot about the film development process today because of the digital age we live in. However, the same method once used to develop film to preserve and prevent it from being destroyed provides a good example of how the Word of God allows us to filter out the deceptive lights of the Devil.

Darkroom printing paper has a sensitivity to **blue light**, so darkrooms are set up to avoid that particular color in the visible light spectrum. Using a safelight with a **red filter** helps prevent any blue light from coming through and affecting the development of the photo paper. That's how the light of the word of God works! When we compare our thoughts, and the thoughts and suggestions that the world impresses upon us, to the light of His word, His word filters out all the lies so we can see the real picture!

> Throwing down imaginations and every high thing that is exalted against the knowledge of God and *bringing every thought into captivity to the obedience of Christ* and being in readiness to avenge all disobedience when your obedience is made full. (2 Corinthians 10:5-6, WEB)

We are to compare everything to the Truth of God's word in order to filter out the lies and align our thoughts to His thoughts. The lies of the Devil are his greatest weapons. He will lie to you about your identity — who God created you to be. He will lie to you about other people to sow discord. He will lie to you about your circumstances to rob you of hope. He will lie to you about your future to prevent you from following your destiny. He will lie to you about your health. He will lie to you about your spouse, children, co-workers, and boss — on and on he lies! Jesus tells us how to get free from those lies, He says, "If you abide in my word, you are truly my disciples, and you will know the truth, and the truth will set you free" (John 8:31-32, WEB).

The truth will set us free from the lies the enemy uses to keep us in darkness and bondage. Let's go into the darkroom and filter out all those artificial lights the enemy wants to use to destroy the perfect picture God has created, so we can discern the truth.

Blue Lights

Let's start with those blue lights. As I was researching blue lights, I found something that just boggled my mind. Our smartphones, tablets, laptops, and TVs give off a **blue light!** In fact, we are cautioned to not be on our phones, or using our computers, or watching TV before we go to bed because the blue light affects our sleep. Isn't that wild? A **blue light!** No wonder so many cannot find their way, we are just as entranced by the blue lights as the turtles are! How many people today are being influenced by their screens? People spend hours on their phones, tablets, and computers, scrolling social media, getting sucked into the latest news cycle, or binging movies and television! Think about all those blue lights Satan is using to mislead us.

Hear me: I'm not saying that everything we watch is of the devil, or that those devices are of the Devil; what I am saying, is that we are being influenced more by *the lights **in** the world* than we are by *the light **of** the world* —Jesus, the Word of God. A recent study revealed that the average American spends 1,642 hours a year watching TV, and 608 hours a year on social media. That adds up to 2,250 hours. The average American only has about 2,920 hours of free time per year after work and sleep. Subtract the average 2,250 hours that are spent in front of blue lights from the 2,920 total hours you have, and you are left with a balance of 670 hours for the year! That means most Americans spend about 77 percent of their free time being influenced by the blue lights of the world and not by *the Light of the word!*

I saw a documentary about how most social media companies

operate. They talked about how all the social media sites collect your information from the sites you visit, and the movies and video's you watch —these are called "cookies." These cookies go into a database governed by a computer that uses something called Artificial Intelligence (A.I.). This computer begins to profile you using all the data it has collected about you. Then, big marketing companies and political parties pay these social media companies to send you ads and videos, in an effort to get you to buy things you don't need, or to persuade you to change your political views to achieve their agenda. Whether you're aware of it or not, companies, political parties, and news outlets are talking to you through these social media platforms. So much fear is being produced from all the media. I think the Bible reflects this in Luke, "It will seem like all hell has broken loose—sun, moon, stars, earth, sea, in an uproar and *everyone all over the world in a panic*, the wind knocked out of them by the threat of doom, the powers-that-be quaking (Luke 21:25-26, MSG).

A programmer for one of those big companies said, "You need to know the **truth** to protect yourself from everything that is presented to you from these social media platforms." My jaw hit the floor! Here is a guy telling us, from a secular perspective, that the lies are so great and so deceptive that you need the **truth** to protect you! He went on to say how billions of people will have thoughts, suggestions, and imaginings that they never would have had if they had not spent so much time following these social media sites, these lights in the world.

Let's take a look at just one of the known damaging effects of these blue lights:

- Recent studies show that 34% of internet users have experienced unwanted exposure to pornographic content through ads, pop-up ads, misdirected links or emails.
- 35% of all internet downloads are related to pornography.
- According to a 2010 report from the National Coalition for the Protection of Children & Families, 47% of families in the United States reported that pornography is a problem in their home.
- The porn industry's annual revenue is more than the NFL, NBA, and MLB combined. It is also more than the combined revenues of ABC, CBS, and NBC.
- 57% of pastors say porn addiction is the most damaging issue in their congregation. 69% say porn has adversely impacted the church.

I'm not even going to get started with how many pastors are struggling with pornography, but I will say that I heard a statistic that 75 percent of pastors do not make themselves accountable to anyone for their Internet use. That is a recipe for disaster when we consider how vital accountability of all kinds is in safeguarding the lives of believers.

These blue lights can also rob us of our creativity, especially our children. If they spend all their time playing video games and surfing apps, they are not exploring their talents, gifts, and abilities — they aren't using their skills to create and imagine. They can also be deprived of developing positive social skills. I've noticed how my grandchildren express their creativity with building blocks, toys, and activities when they are not on their tablets or phones. They engage more in board games, and crafts, and sports. When we allow our children to over-indulge in the blue lights, we are keeping them from discovering their God-given talents and abilities.

Blinding Lights

"Satan, who is the god of this world, has blinded the minds of those who don't believe." They are unable to see the glorious light of the Good News. They don't understand this message about the glory of Christ, who is the exact likeness of God." (2 Corinthians 4:4, TPT)

Unbelievers can't see the truth because they don't trust in the God who is shining the light along the way that leads to life. What is happening in the world today, even among believers, is that they have been blinded by all the other lights! It's not that they are truly blind, but that they have been blinded by Satan's lies that appear to be true!

> "They promise them liberty, when they themselves are the slaves of depravity—for by whatever anyone is defeated *and* overcome, to that [person, thing, philosophy, or concept] he is *continually* enslaved." (2 Peter 2:19, AMP)

Even in the Christian community, truth is becoming less visible for the sake of avoiding offending someone or hurting their feelings. As a result, we've watered down the truth with quotes like, "love covers sins" or "love covers bible verses," and sayings of that nature. We have to avoid removing any sense of conviction because we don't want anyone to feel uncomfortable.

Sometimes change is necessary. We should be asking ourselves, "What will those people outside the church think about us on the day of judgement when they are judged by the truth of God's word?" Another question for us to consider is, "What will God say to us in regard to how we upheld the truth?" Now, love does *cover* sin — by washing it away in the grace of God! But love does not *excuse* sin. We have to be careful not to accidentally wash away Jesus from our redemption story by watering down the Gospel!

Paul says in his letter:

> What shall we say then? *Shall we continue in sin, that grace may abound? May it never be*! We who died to sin, how could we live in it any longer? Or don't you know that all we who were baptized into Christ Jesus were baptized into his death? We were buried therefore with him through baptism into death that just as Christ was raised from the dead through the glory of the Father, *so we also might walk in newness of life.*

> For if we have become united with him in the likeness of his death, we will also be part of his resurrection; knowing this, that our old sin was crucified with him, *that the body of sin might be done away with, so that we would no longer be in bondage to sin.* For he who has died has been freed from sin. (Romans 6:1-7, WEB)

In light of what Paul wrote to the church in Rome, God's plan is to set us free from sin through our salvation, and He does! There is no comfortable way to tell someone they need to die to the way they are living if they want to be saved and find the plans and purposes God has for their life. To say, "Love covers Bible verses," is often interpreted to mean, "It doesn't matter what the Bible says about sin, or certain behaviors, because God's love covers you." But let me share why that kind of thinking is not only wrong, but dangerous. First, it goes back to needing that foundational truth to make sane decisions. Secondly, the word of God is God's light telling us which way to go, not to control us, but to avoid danger!

Here is an example: I have several grandchildren, and some of them are toddlers. Now, if one of them runs out to the road (sometimes they do just take off in any direction), I will yell out "stop!" (While I'm running after them) or "Get back over here!" My words are being spoken in love, even if they sound harsh! Because I love them, I'm going to tell them what they need to hear and not what they want to hear. When we water down teaching to tell people what they want to hear, it miscommunicates the love of God. God doesn't change His commands to avoid hurting our feelings, because His commands keep us from hurting ourselves. Bottom line, this verse from Psalms shines the light on what I'm saying,

> "Your word is a lamp to my feet, and a light for my path." (Psalm 119:105, WEB)

God's word outshines all the other lights. Don't allow the lights of the Devil's deception to blind you from *"The Light"* of God.

Mirage Lights

Mirage lights are the people who pose as sheep (i.e., believers) but are actually wolves in sheep's clothing. Jesus warns us:

> Beware of false prophets, who come to you in sheep's clothing, but inwardly are ravening wolves. By their fruits you will know them. (Matthew 7:15-17, WEB)

Notice He said the false prophets are "sheep disguised as wolves." False prophets are not the Shepherds. It's the people in the "flock" that you have to watch out for! Listen to the words of the apostle Paul to the church in Galatia:

> You were running well! Who interfered with you that you should not obey the truth? This persuasion is not from him who calls you. A little yeast grows through the whole lump. (Galatians 5:7-10, WEB)

Sometimes it is the people in the church that are leading us astray. We may be prepared to avoid the "blue lights" of the world's distractions, and the "blinding lights" of Satan's deceptions, but completely caught off guard by the "mirage lights," the misdirection of other believers. And what's more is these believers lead us astray *because* they are following the other lights, believing they are going the right way!

These believers may be misguided because they are not following the *red light* of the word; or they may know the word, but they are not applying it to their own lives, lying to themselves. The writers of the Passion translation nailed it:

> "Don't just listen to the Word of Truth and not respond to it, for that is the essence of self-deception. So always let his Word become like poetry written and fulfilled by your life!" (James 1:22, TPT)

Here are some examples of things I ran into early in my Christian walk that really threw me off. I have met so many professing believers that claim there is nothing wrong with sex outside of marriage, or drugs, or alcohol, or any number of other sins. However, when you line it up with the word of God you get a conflicting perspective. Paul says in his letter to Corinth:

> Don't you know that the unrighteous will not inherit God's Kingdom? Don't be deceived. Neither the sexually immoral, nor idolaters, nor adulterers, nor male prostitutes, nor homosexuals, nor thieves, nor covetous, nor drunkards, nor slanderers, nor extortionists, will inherit God's Kingdom. (2 Corinthians 6:9-10 WEB)

I could have saved myself a lot of self-deceptions if I would have compared what people *claim* to be true, to "*the truth*" of God's word. We have to make sure the people that we allow into our lives are not misleading us. Listen to what Jesus says:

Not everyone who says to me, "Lord, Lord," will enter into the Kingdom of Heaven, but he who does the will of my Father who is in heaven. Many will tell me in that day, "Lord, Lord, didn't we prophesy in your name, in your name cast out demons, and in your name do many mighty works?" Then I will tell them, "I never knew you. Depart from me, you who work iniquity." (Matthew 7:21-23, WEB)

Isn't that sobering?! So many claim that Jesus is their Lord, and yet they do not do what He says! The apostle Paul also instructs us to be careful who we associate with, saying,

"***Do not be misled***: Bad Company corrupts good character. (1 Corinthians 15:33, NLT)

Perhaps why God often refers to us as sheep is because we can be so easily influenced and misled. Many people say sheep are stupid; don't get offended — wait until you see where I'm going with this. I read somewhere (I can't remember exactly where, or the exact words, but it left an impression), about how sheep have no sense of direction – at all. As a result, they will follow whoever is leading them, even if it leads them off a cliff! There was an accident in Eastern Turkey where about 1500 unattended sheep fell off a cliff while the shepherds were eating breakfast far away from the flock. The first 400 fell to their death in a ravine — the remaining 1100 were saved because the first 400 broke the fall for the others.

I would imagine that the sheep in back could see no further than the sheep in front of them, so they were unaware of what was ahead. I would also suggest the sheep in front couldn't stop when they did see danger because the sheep in the back were pushing them forward. Some might find this image a little comical, and those who are more sensitive may get a little emotional over the incident. But don't miss the point, and don't think too highly of yourself; the reality is that we all can be just as easily misled.

Years ago, I met an elderly Christian man who later became a mentor to me in the faith. He shared with me how, when he was younger, he was sitting in a church pew when out of nowhere, it felt like someone put their hand on his chest and pressed the breath out of him. He went on to say that suddenly he was seeing a vision of people walking toward a cliff and falling into a pit of fire! He said there were so many people crowding each other that, by the time they got to the edge, they couldn't turn back!

We need teachers and preachers (shepherds), to tell us the truth no matter how much it hurts, offends, or inconveniences us. The danger I see today is that we are so afraid of offending someone with the truth that we shrink away from it, even when sharing the truth that could save their life. God rejected the priests for not telling the people the truth. He said through the prophet Hosea, *"My people are destroyed for lack of knowledge* [of My law, where I reveal My will]. Because you [the priestly nation] have rejected knowledge, I will also reject you from being My priest" (Hosea 4:6, AMP). We need to be a people who tell the truth in love. Neither allow yourself to be led astray by these mirage lights, nor be the one who leads another astray by shrinking back from the truth.

Light or Lights?

Jesus warns us of the dangers of following the lights that shine on the wrong path. In Matthew's gospel, He says:

> Enter in by the narrow gate; for the gate is wide and the way is broad that leads to destruction, and there are **many** who enter in by it. Because the gate is narrow and the way is restricted that leads to life! **Few** are those who find it. (Matthew 7:13-14, WEB)

The lights in the world, blue, blinding, and mirage alike, mislead so many. In fact, the word *"many"* in verse 13 above in the Greek means the "majority!" How tragic that the majority of people are misled and only a few find the life God has for them. To continue our word study, the Greek word for *"life"* in this passage is "Zoe" – it's the abundant life, a life as God would have it, a full life, a life with nothing held back. This life is found only in God.

Jesus came so that you could have that life! Listen to His words, "A thief has only one thing in mind—he wants to steal, slaughter, and destroy. But I have come to *give you everything in abundance, more than you expect* — life in its fullness until you overflow" (John 10:10, TPT). This is the life God desires for you to have! That is truth! However, the sobering reality is that Matthew 7's message is also true — only a *few* find it. Only a few make it to the waters of their destiny, God's best for their lives!

The *majority* are led astray by the lies of the devil, those deceiving lights. The devil promises that the way to life can be found traveling on the freeway, the freeway of this world. The freeway follows a life that pleases and satisfies the passions and pleasures of the flesh, "our fallen nature." But the Devil doesn't want us to know about the dangers of the freeway that can lead to destruction. Because we can be deceived so easily by the desires of our own flesh, we end up missing all the danger signs. I love the way The Message translates this verse,

> "How can a young person live a clean life? By carefully reading the map of your Word. I'm single-minded in pursuit of you; don't let me miss the road signs you've posted." (Psalms 119:11, MSG)

There is only one way to life, the narrow way, the difficult way, against the grain. Trying to find fulfillment, pleasure, satisfaction, and purpose following along the freeway of this world always ends in disappointment, despair, disillusionment, and ultimately destruction. The abundant life God offers is a life found in Him, along His path. It's not found among the flashiness of money, or material things, or a job or title. Jesus tells us to be on guard against that kind of thinking.

> "Beware! Keep yourselves from covetousness, for a man's life doesn't consist of the abundance of the things which he possesses." (Luke 12:15, WEB)

The abundant Life is found in a relationship with Him, and He will take care of our needs when our focus is on Him, and His path, and not on the things of this world. So many cannot find the abundant life because they are searching for it in the wrong places and things.

When the many artificial lights along the Devil's freeway vie for our attention, we need to keep our eyes focused on *The Light* of truth, and travel on God's path for us, which is a one-way street from the moment of redemption.

Solomon said, "*Buy the truth*, and sell it not; also, wisdom, and instruction, and understanding" (Proverbs 23:23). Here's how you "buy the truth," *you sell all the lies you have bought.*

CHARTER GUIDE TWO
"The Light of the World or the Lights in the World"

Your second choice is to follow the light *of the world* or the lights *in the world.*

- Reflect on a time when you thought you were going in the right direction by following a dream, or a goal, or a relationship, or some other thing, only to discover you were going in the wrong direction.

- What do you believe about the objective truth of the Bible, to which you can compare all your thoughts, ideas, emotions and distractions of the world?

- What does it mean to you that God's word is the infallible truth, and that Jesus is our guiding light?

- How have you been misled at times by the blue lights of social media, internet, or TV?

- What do you sacrifice in order to spend time under the influence of the blue lights of the world?

- How do you prepare yourself to guard against the blinding lights of Satan that aim to hide the truth?

- Describe a time you have been misled by Christians. How did it affect your walk with God and others?

- Has knowing the truth changed your life?

THE CHOICE

You have the choice: to either follow the *light of the world* or the *lights in the world.*

Scripture: "Truth's shining light guides me in my choices and decisions; the revelation of your Word makes my pathway clear." (Psalm 119:105, TPT)

Thought: Your destiny hinges on what you believe to be truth.

NOTES:

Choice Three

Deep or Shallow Waters

O nce those hatchlings locked eyes on the red light, they followed it with total abandonment to the sea. They had no regard for the life they were leaving behind. Imagine what would happen if they followed the light all the way to the *edge* of the sea but did not get in the water! What if, instead they tried to live *close* to the water without getting *into* the water? Jesus warned that there would be people who would see the light, but would not enter the waters of the will of the Father. They would know what to do but would not do it. They did not follow the light with total abandonment, leaving behind the things of this world. I hit on this a little with Choice Two, but let's look again at Jesus' words in Matthew:

> Not everyone who says to me, "Lord, Lord," will enter into the Kingdom of Heaven, but he who

does the will of my Father who is in heaven. Many will tell me in that day, "Lord, Lord, didn't we prophesy in your name, in your name cast out demons, and in your name do many mighty works?" Then I will tell them, "I never knew you. Depart from me, you who work iniquity." (Matthew 7:21-23, WEB)

Imagine the Ocean is the judge of the sea turtles. After they die, their relationship with the Ocean will determine whether they will spend eternity on land, in the scorching heat of the sun, or in the sea, saturated in the endless bliss and provision of the Ocean. Now, let's say there is a large group that saw the red light but never followed it to the water, so they eventually die on land. In a world where sea turtles face their own Day of Judgment, they come before the Ocean to give an account of their lives. The Ocean says, "I never knew you," even though they are *sea* turtles! The Ocean goes onto explain its decision by saying, "You never lived in the "waters" for which you were created!" It's the same with the people in this passage. Even though they were created in the image of God and knew the truth about Jesus as the Light of the truth of God's word, they did not allow the word of God to be the final authority in their lives. In rejecting this authority, they did not live the life they were created for.

We read in James's letter, "But be doers of the word, and not only hearers, *deluding* your own selves" (James 1:22, WEB). Strong's defines the Greek word "delude," as deceive, beguile, reason falsely, *mislead*. We can actually *mislead* ourselves by knowing the truth and not doing it! Remember, the inability to make a decision based on truth is our working definition of insanity. Notice, one of the ways Strong's defines delude is to *reason falsely*. Then, and now, there are those who know the Word, preach the Word, perform miracles with the Word, but *reason* independent from the Word. They have never made the Word of God the final authority over their lives, therefore their actions do not line up with the truth. They did not live the way the Creator created them to live and could not thrive.

In the Shallows

I used to be just like those who *heard*, but did not *do*, and yet thought they were on their way to heaven! I grew up in church, and I even remember saying to my mother how I felt God wanted me to preach. However, after the death of my father I became bitter toward God. I was very rebellious at home, at school and with any authority. As a teenager, I started getting into drugs, alcohol, fights, stealing, and sexual sin. I was very angry, and I was in and out of detention centers and drug and alcohol rehab centers. I remember getting so angry at God that I made a new year's resolution that I would *never* serve Him! At one point, I cursed Him in every way imaginable.

After years of abusing my body, the drugs and rough living began to take its toll on me. I wondered if there was any way I could be forgiven after all the things I said to God and the oath I took never to serve Him. God is so merciful, even beyond our comprehension. He answered my silent prayers — sending people my way to witness to me about the grace of God. As a result, I began my journey back to Him and I was even baptized. But this is not a story of baptism followed by "Happily Ever

After." Once I was baptized, my Christian walk was more like a roller coaster ride. I was so bound by my addictions that I would get clean, go to church, then relapse. I did this over and over, journeying deeper into sin with each relapse. The final straw came after an overdose of pills and alcohol where I almost died. Only God knows exactly what happened that day. Some think I was hit by a car — left for dead. All I remember is waking up in a puddle of blood. My head was swollen to the size of a basketball. My teeth had pierced my lips and I felt that my wrists were broken. Whatever the circumstances were that led me to that place, I felt like that was God's cry to me: "It's time to wake up!"

Again, don't expect my whole story to come together tied up neatly with a bow in this next paragraph. Follow me all the way through. I joined a small church and started all over again (for the hundredth time). Once again, I began to experience the mercy of God; I was reading the Bible, I found a job, and I was staying away from the drugs. I had even experienced the baptism of the Holy Spirit, which had never happened to me before. Yet, somewhere along the way, my addictions and insane reasoning got the better of me. As I mentioned earlier, some of my delusions about grace were formed by the teachings of others who claimed to be Christians —I was allowing myself to be misled. These people I trusted claimed you could live however you wanted to live and still be saved. But I didn't know that Jesus not only died to forgive me of my sin, but also died to deliver me from the *power* of my sin. What I believed during that season was: I was saved, but I had no control over the desires of my flesh.

I knew what scripture said in Matthew 7:21, but I had come

to a place where I did not think that those words applied to me. I believed His love was now covering my sin, so I could go on sinning! That is what I believed! I believed that God would only look at the blood of Jesus, not my sinful passions — for me, that was how salvation worked. I reasoned that there was no way to combat my fleshly appetites, and that God understood that. He would just cover my sinful behaviors (I had the love covers verses mentality I talked about in Choice Two). I started using drugs, sleeping around, and committing all the sins I had before and worse! This is not only hard to confess, it's hard just to write it down as the honest truth! As the years go by, and as I understand the grace of God more, I wonder what I was even thinking, and how I could have come to this conclusion! There were times I would feel some conviction and try to make little changes; but the addictions, and the way I viewed salvation, would cloud my reasoning. It was interesting though, regardless of how I justified continuing to live in sin, because of the work of the Holy Spirit in my life, living in sin was no longer the same. The drugs, and so forth, did not seem to bring the pleasure they did before. Despite all the work of the Holy Spirit in my life I continued to believe that God loved us and as long as you believed that you were saved! Listen to what the Holy Spirit says through Paul:

> Now the deeds of the flesh are obvious, which are: adultery, sexual immorality, uncleanness, lustfulness, idolatry, sorcery, hatred, strife, jealousies, and outbursts of anger, rivalries, divisions, heresies, envy, murders, drunkenness, orgies, and things like these; of which I forewarn

you, even as I also forewarned you, that those who practice such things will not inherit God's Kingdom. (Galatians 5:19-21, WEB)

That summed me up! And notice it there in black and white: if we live like that, we will not enter the kingdom! I was right about one thing, however: I was (and still am) God's child. God disciplines his children. The writer of Hebrews says, "My son, don't take lightly the chastening of the Lord, nor faint when you are reproved by him; for *whom the Lord loves, he disciplines, and chastises every son whom he receives.*" (Hebrews 12:5-6, WEB)

Notice the word *love*. I've heard it said that *discipline is the highest form of love*. God definitely loved me, and He was about to demonstrate His love for this child! During that season of my life, I knew a lady, the daughter of a pastor, who was sharing her testimony with me. In the conversation, she started quoting John 3:16, "For God so loved the world that he gave his one and only Son, that whoever believes in him should not perish, but have eternal life" (WEB). Amazingly, as she was quoting John 3:16, God was quoting to me a passage from Hebrews:

For if we sin willfully after we have received the knowledge of the truth, there remains no more a sacrifice for sins, but a certain fearful expectation of judgment, and a fierceness of fire which will devour the adversaries. A man who disregards Moses' law dies without compassion on the word of two or three witnesses. How much worse punishment, do you think, will he be judged worthy of, who has trodden underfoot the Son of God, and has counted the blood of the covenant with which he was sanctified an unholy thing, and has insulted the Spirit of grace? (Hebrews 10:26-29, WEB)

Not only were those verses running through my mind, but I was also seeing in a vision how I had trampled the son of God underfoot! In that moment, I felt like I was standing in the presence of eternity without a prayer! I was so terrified that I just wanted to run! Imagine all the things there are to fear in life: war, natural disasters, persecution, terrorism — whatever your worst nightmares are. Even combined, that fear pales in comparison to what I felt that day. I can tell you from experience that the most terrifying feeling in the world is to stand before God without Christ!

> "For we know the one who said, 'I will take revenge. I will pay them back.' He also said, 'The LORD will judge his own people.' It is a terrible thing to fall into the hands of the living God" (Hebrews 10:30-31, WEB). God will judge His people! When He disciplines us in this life, it is to save us from being condemned with the world. After we die, His judgement is final. "But when we are judged, we are punished by the Lord, that we may not be condemned with the world" (1 Corinthians 11:32, WEB).

God's discipline is proof that we are His children. In fact, if God is not correcting you, the Bible says you are not His child (Heb. 12:8). The day after God spoke into my heart from Hebrews 10. I was so shook-up by the experience that I just wanted to run away from Christianity. As I was thinking about running away, suddenly I felt like I was once again standing *in* eternity. I don't know how else to describe it. It was frightening. There was nowhere to run from the presence of God; I could literally feel His physical presence taking up the whole space. Then I heard God speak these words, *"where will you run?"* I had no response to give. Then He said, *"Warn them."* I knew He meant the people who thought and believed the way I did, who were living a lifestyle deep in sin while claiming to be a Christian.

One of my favorite preachers and authors is John Bevere; his teaching played a major role in my walk with God. I remember a vision John talked about that was given to him from the Lord: he was looking out at a sea of people. He could not see where they ended in any direction. He could not see the people at the end in the back, or side to side. It was like an ocean of people, beyond the sight line of the horizon. He says the Lord was standing near him and said to him, "John, all these people think they are going to hear 'enter into the joy of the Lord,' but instead they are going to hear 'depart from me.'"

The unsettling thing about his vision is that it lines up with the words of Jesus when He said many professing believers (not pagans, atheists, agnostics, etc.), will hear those words! If it were not for the grace of God, I believe I would have been in that sea of people!

> ***Many*** will tell me in that day, "Lord, Lord, didn't we prophesy in your name, in your name cast

out demons, and in your name do many mighty works?" Then I will tell them, "I never knew you. Depart from me, you who work iniquity." (Matthew 7:22-23, WEB)

We have to not only believe *in* God, but *believe* God. James tells us that if we know the word and don't do what it says, we deceive ourselves. "Do not merely listen to the *word,* and so *deceive yourselves.* Do what it says." (James 1:22, NIV)

It's been said that Jesus cannot save anyone He cannot command. Listen to Paul's warning to the church,

> For I do not want you to be ignorant of the fact, brothers and sisters, that our ancestors were all under the cloud and that they all passed through the sea. They were all baptized into Moses in the cloud and in the sea. They all ate the same spiritual food and drank the same spiritual drink; for they drank from the spiritual rock that accompanied them, and that rock was Christ. Nevertheless, God was not pleased with most of them; their bodies were scattered in the wilderness.
>
> Now these things occurred as examples to keep us from setting our hearts on evil things as they did. Do not be idolaters, as some of them were, as it is written: "The people sat down to eat and drink and got up to indulge in revelry. We should not commit sexual immorality, as some of them

did—and in one day twenty-three thousand of them died. We should not test Christ, as some of them did—and were killed by snakes. And do not grumble, as some of them did—and were killed by the destroying angel.

These things happened to them as examples and were written down *"as warnings for us,"* on whom the culmination of the ages has come. (1 Corinthians 10:1-11, WEB)

I did not understand everything about grace at once, and I'm still learning. It has taken me years to understand the truths I *do* know. In fact, I did not start preaching and teaching until almost 14 years after this experience, and even then, not as a pastor. I would preach and teach only when there was an opportunity for me. As I write this book, it has been a little over 22 years since my journey began.

As God was dealing with me back then about the way I was living and believing; I felt so broken and condemned. I didn't know if I could go on, let alone how to move forward. I questioned if I could ever be forgiven. Let me tell you what I learned — you can be forgiven no matter how far down you have gone. "If we confess our sins, *he is faithful and righteous to forgive us the sins*, and to cleanse us from all unrighteousness" (John 1:9, WEB).

During this season I was at church one morning talking with the Pastors wife. Because I was feeling so lost and so broken, I began to share with her what I was going through. She was so wise; she did not miss a beat! She said, *"Before*

Jesus blessed anything — He broke it!" after she said that I was so moved by those words that I ran to a bathroom to hide my tears. I realized that it was the grace and mercy of God working in my life, restoring me. "The sacrifices of God are a broken spirit. O God, you will not despise a broken and contrite heart" (Psalm 51:17, WEB). The Hebrew meaning for the word "broken" in this passage means "to brake, crush, or destroy." We have to allow ourselves to be broken by our sins, and I learned through my journey that brokenness cannot happen until we know the depth of our sin.

Going Deep

I wish I could say I woke up one morning and never struggled with sin again, but that is not the reality — for anyone! What I needed was to learn the *depth* of my sin; that's where true brokenness begins. The Bible says on the day of Pentecost that the people were *"cut to the heart"* by the words of Peter.

> "Let all the house of Israel therefore know certainly that God has made him both Lord and Christ, this Jesus *whom you crucified."* Now when they heard this, they were *cut to the heart*, and said to Peter and the rest of the apostles, "Brothers, what shall we do?" (Acts 2:36-37, WEB)

The imagery of being cut shows their feelings of deep conviction, as they realized that they were guilty of killing their own Messiah. The conviction of sin is often the missing ingredient in our messages today. The big eye-opening moment for me was when I realized it was *my* sin that drove the nails in Jesus hands. I've heard it said that if you don't know the *depth* of your sin, you don't have a real Savior on the cross. I agree with that, and the reason is because we have a way of putting sin in a box.

Consider the way we view certain sins as "worse" than others. For example, some might say drugs and alcohol are bad, but having sex outside of marriage is understandable, or you might hear condemnation of those who are pathological liars, but also see that half-truths are accepted (even though, as I've always been told, a "half-truth" is a "whole lie"). We know not to steal, but maybe cheating a little on your taxes is ok. All these examples, (and there are countless more), are shallow; they just scratch the surface of sin. We will be tempted to believe this way until we are *cut deep* by the word!

Jesus pointed out it is the sick that need a doctor, "Those who are healthy have no need for a physician, but those who are sick" (Mark 2:17, WEB). Here is the flip side of that truth: if you don't know you are sick, you are not going to seek a doctor! We are too quick to try and heal people of their illness (sin) when they do not yet realize that they are sick (apart from God)! We have to allow them to be wounded in their conscience so they will seek the medical attention of the Healer.

"For the word of God is quick, and powerful, and *sharper than any two-edged sword*, piercing even to the dividing asunder of soul and spirit, and of the joints and marrow, and is a discerner of the thoughts and intents of the heart" (Hebrews 4:12, KJV). We must be cut by the word so we can see the infection of sin in us; that is when real change occurs. In my vision, I was seeing my sin for the first time in the light of a Holy

God, just like the crowd on the day of Pentecost. I want to point out that the people who were cut by the words of Peter were more than likely religious people! These were not people who were strung out on drugs, lost deep in sin like I was, but rather these were everyday people who probably went to synagogue meetings, paid their tithes, and looked after their families, and so on. But when they realized that it was *their* sin that crucified Jesus, they were cut deep.

After they were cut by the word, they asked, "What shall we do?" and Peter replies,

"Repent, and be baptized, every one of you, in the name of Jesus Christ for the forgiveness of sins, and you will receive the gift of the Holy Spirit" (Acts 2:38, WEB).

It seems that many messages today consist more of "believe and you will be saved." Somewhere along the way we lost touch with the word "repent." Repent is almost seen as a negative word, and we view it that way because it has been used to beat people into submission instead of leading them to freedom in Christ. Repentance is not bondage; it is what leads us to *freedom from our bondage* to sin!

When we repent, God saturates us with His presence and power. Peter said, "Repent therefore, and turn again, that your sins may be blotted out, so that there may come times of refreshing from the presence of the Lord" (Acts 2:19, WEB). What an awesome promise! In spite of this promise, it seems today we want to *cover* sin rather than to *cleanse* sin. We read in Proverbs, "There is a generation that is pure in their own eyes yet are *not washed from their filthiness*" (Proverbs 30:12, WEB). **Too often, we put a bandage on sin and call it cleansed.** We cover the wound but ignore the infection! We then wait, hoping it will heal on its own. Cleaning an infection can be a painful process, and we don't want to make people uncomfortable.

I was jogging around my neighborhood late one afternoon when a dog came seemingly out of nowhere and bit me on the leg. I went to a clinic to have it checked, and the nurse pulled out a syringe and said she was going to clean the wound. There was no needle involved (thankfully), but she did use a solution and shot the solution into the puncture wound with the syringe. It was definitely not a comfortable feeling, but, if I had not endured the treatment of the cleansing process, the infection would have spread throughout my body. It is the same with sin — it will only continue to spread if it's not treated. The process of cleansing yourself from a pattern of sin may involve breaking off an unhealthy relationship or changing jobs because the current environment tempts you to fall back into sin, or going to someone and admitting you were wrong. These are all a part of the cleansing process of repentance. Repentance is the outward evidence of a change of mind.

Paul said, "I declared first to them of Damascus, at Jerusalem, and throughout all the country of Judea, and also to the Gentiles, that they should *repent* and *turn to God, doing works worthy of repentance"* (Acts 26:20, WEB). There are two types of repentance: One says, "I'm sorry I sinned, and it breaks *my* heart." The other says, "I'm sorry I sinned, and broke *your* heart." It's only when we realize we have broken the heart of God that we have reached true repentance.

The lives of Peter and Judas paint a picture for us of what the two types of repentance look like. The Bible says, When Peter realized he had denied Jesus three times (as the Lord predicted), he was close enough to Jesus to make eye contact; when he saw Jesus, he ran and wept for what he had done. The Lord turned and looked at Peter. Then Peter remembered the Lord's word, how he said to him, "Before the rooster crows you will deny me three times. *He went out and wept bitterly"* (Luke 22:61-62, WEB). Peter was broken by his sin when he realized it had infected His relationship with his Master; he was cut deep, and he wept bitterly.

When Judas realized he had betrayed Jesus, he went out and hung himself (Matthew 27:5), because his relationship with the Master wasn't the focus. We have all heard stories of men and women who are caught in a sinful act and commit suicide, having been exposed. For some reason, they would rather end their lives than to face their guilt and work to restore their relationships. Repentance can actually be viewed as a **selfless** act, because they are seeking to restore their relationship with God, and others, no matter how much it hurts. Choosing death over repentance could be seen as a **selfish** act, because they don't want to go through the cleansing process of repentance to restore the relationship with God and others, no matter how much their loss hurts others.

When it comes to repentance, you have to choose to dive in deep for true repentance or stay in the comforts of the shallows of your sin. As I write, I have been drug free for 22 years, and have been delivered from a number of other vices during that time (by the grace of God). The Lord led me to a godly woman, who I later married. We have two adult children, who are in the faith, and six grandchildren. I have served for years in full time ministry working with men seeking to change their lives. Not to mention I have written a book! I would have to write a whole other book to talk about the things I have seen God do in my life, and in the lives of others over the years! I live every day with an indescribable peace and joy in my spirit, and I know all this is a result of being in a relationship with God through Christ. Be encouraged, for He says, "At an acceptable time I listened to you. In a day of salvation, I helped you. Behold, now is the acceptable time. Behold, now is the day of salvation" (1 Corinthians 6:2, WEB). Take it from me: it is much better to be like the hatchlings who followed the red light and dove into the unknown depths of the sea for which they were created. Don't allow yourself to be content watching from the edge of the water. Dive in and experience your Creator.

CHARTER GUIDE THREE
"Deep or Shallow Waters"

Your third choice is to go *deep in repentance* or stay in the *comforts of the shallows*.

- Reflect on the ways you have been self-deceived, living a life that contradicts the teachings of Jesus.

- Have you ever been "cut deep" by the word of God or by the Spirit of God? What was that experience like?

- What has your personal experience been with repentance? Do you feel it brought liberty, or condemnation?

- What do you see is the difference between God's correction and His condemnation?

- How has your life changed as a result of repentance?

THE CHOICE

You have to choose to *go deep in repentance* or *stay in the comforts of the shallows.*

Scripture: Peter said, "Repent therefore, and turn again, that your sins may be blotted out, so that there may come times of refreshing from the presence of the Lord" (Acts 2:19, WEB).

Thought: I've heard it said that if you don't know the *depth* of your sin, you don't have a real Savior on the cross.

NOTES:

Choice Four

Castles of Stone or Castles of Sand

E veryone, therefore, who hears these words of mine and does them, I will liken him to a wise man who built his house on a rock. The rain came down, the floods came, and the winds blew and beat on that house; and it didn't fall, for it was founded on the rock. Everyone who hears these words of mine and doesn't do them will be like a foolish man who built his house on the sand. The rain came down, the floods came, and the winds blew and beat on that house; and it fell—and its fall was great. (Matthew 7:21-27, WEB)

Due to storms, hurricanes, and changing weather patterns, nesting grounds for sea turtles are not always safe. Since sea turtles plant their eggs on the beaches in the sand the nests can be easily washed away during storms. These storms actually test the structure and durability of the nests. Jesus forecasts that, in our lives, there will be storms. If we don't have a solid foundation for our lives when the storms of life come, our lives will be washed away like the weakest of the sea turtle nests.

Years ago, I heard a story of a house in Florida that survived a hurricane. It was back in 1992 when Andrew, a powerful hurricane, hit southern Florida; it literally leveled thousands of homes. In most areas the devastation and destruction were so total it looked like there had been a nuclear war, but one of the houses remained firmly anchored on its foundation. A reporter asked the homeowner why his house had not been destroyed. The homeowner's words still ring my ears today "I built this house myself. I also built it according to the Florida state building code. When the code called for 2x6 roof trusses, I used 2x6 roof trusses. I was told that a house built according to code could withstand a hurricane - and it did." I just love the simplicity of his testimony —he just built it according to code, using the materials required. That's it! The blueprints for how we are to build our lives are equally as clear. We build them according to the "code" written in the word of God!

The storms in life test us, and often expose what we have built our lives on. If we build our lives on wealth, power, popularity, position, or the pleasures of life, what happens when those things are washed away? How will you respond when the storms come? Our last choice challenged us to look at the dangers of not doing what the word of God says, which would be like choosing to build a house without a proper foundation. Our next choice examines our foundation and prepares us for *how* to build upon it.

The Foundation

Let's begin by looking at the foundation we are to build on. Take, for example, the foundation of a house. I have a background in construction, so I'm familiar with the structure and function of a foundation, but I know not everyone is. Every building project needs a solid foundation, because the foundation is what supports the whole structure — walls, flooring, roof, etc... Each foundation is designed specifically for the layout of the structure it will support. Most foundations today are made of concrete, and concrete is made up of three main ingredients. (Yes, before you get ahead of me, with today's technology we can add a variety of elements to concrete. We can add chemicals, entrainment air, fiberglass, and more.) But there are three main elements I want us to focus on (Welcome to Concrete 101). The first ingredient is *stone,* which is an aggregate, and gives strength and durability to the concrete. The second is *cement*, which usually has a lime base, and the third is *water*. All three ingredients play crucial roles in creating a solid foundation.

The Spirit and The Word

The Bible reveals to us that there are also three parts that make up the foundation for our lives. The first two are the *Word*, and the *Spirit*; they are like the *cement* and *water* of our life's foundation. We see this parallel throughout scripture. "It is the spirit who gives life. The flesh profits nothing. The words that I speak to you are *spirit*, and are *life* (John 6:63, WEB). Also recorded in John's gospel, are these words of Jesus,

"Jesus answered, 'Most certainly I tell you, unless one is

born of **water** and **spirit**, he can't enter into God's Kingdom' (John 3:5, WEB).

Let's dig a little deeper here and look at the functions of the **Word** and the **Spirit,** and how they work together. For example, Paul says, "Husbands, love your wives, even as Christ also loved the assembly, and gave himself up for it; that he might sanctify it, having *cleansed* it by the washing of water with the word" (Ephesians 5:25-27).

Jesus also talks about the cleansing power of the word, "You are already *clean* because of the word I have spoken to you" (John 15:3, NIV). We can also see how the word cleanses us in Paul's second letter to Timothy, where he says, "Every Scripture is God-breathed and profitable for *teaching, for reproof, for correction, and for instruction in righteousness*, that each person who belongs to God may be complete, thoroughly equipped for every good work" (2 Timothy 3:16-17, WEB). We see in this passage that the word cleanses us, not literally, but by teaching us right living.

The Word also rebukes us when our thoughts or actions do not line up with the truth. Not only does the Word convict us, but it also guides us to the truth. That is the training process for living right before God. We read in Hebrews, "For the word of God is *living and active,* and sharper than any two-edged sword, piercing even to the dividing of soul and spirit, of both joints and marrow, and is able to discern the thoughts and intentions of the heart (Heb. 4:12, WEB)." Notice the words *living* and *active*. It is the Holy Spirit that brings the word of God to life to penetrate our hearts and minds. Paul writes, "Who also made us sufficient as servants of a new covenant, not of the letter, but of the Spirit. *For the letter kills, but the Spirit gives life"* (2 Cor. 3:6, WEB).

I've met people who know the Bible front to back, and yet their lives remain unchanged. Look at the teachers of the law in Jesus's day, the Pharisees. They had the Old Testament *memorized*, yet their hearts were unchanged. Knowledge of the Word without the action of the Holy Spirit is of no effect. The washing of the Word is a work of the Holy Spirit. He brings the Word to life in our hearts. Judas Iscariot, the betrayer, was washed by the Word, spoken from the mouth of the Savior, and yet remained unchanged. Listen to what Jesus says, "You are already pruned *clean* because of *the word* which I have spoken to you" (John 15:3, WEB). The disciples were washed by the word; however, notice what Jesus says when he washes their feet at the last supper.

"Someone who has bathed only needs to have his feet washed but is completely clean. You are clean, but not all of you" (John 13:10, WEB). *Judas was washed by the Word (Jesus), but he never actually came clean!* He did not make the choice to submit to the Word of the Lord that would cleanse him.

The Stone

"For it stands in Scripture: 'Behold, I am laying in Zion **a stone**, a cornerstone chosen and precious, and whoever *believes* in him will not be put to shame" (1 Peter 2:6, WEB). Without the stone part of the foundation, there is nothing to support the structure. Without the person of Jesus, there would be no one to which the Holy Spirit must bear witness. Jesus's death, burial, and resurrection is what supports the Gospel and the ministry of the Holy Spirit,

Remember, Jesus said the work of the Holy Spirit would begin after He accomplished everything,

> But very truly I tell you, it is for your good that I am going away. *Unless I go away, the Advocate will not come to you; but if I go*, I will *send* him to you...There is so much more I want to tell you, but you can't bear it now. When the Spirit of truth comes, *he will guide you into all truth*. (John 16:12 & 17, NLT)

I love that — *ALL* truth! We need the whole truth for a solid foundation. So, the foundation consists of *believing* in Jesus finished work; his death, burial and resurrection; that is the stone that gives strength and support to the foundation (the message of the Gospel). Then the *Word of God* and *the Spirit of God* are like the cement and water that bond everything together. The apostle Paul describes all three in his letter to the Romans,

> "If you declare with your **mouth** 'Jesus is Lord (*word*),' and **believe** in your heart that God raised him from the dead (*stone*), you will be **saved** (*Spirit*)." (Romans 10:9, NIV, parentheses added)

There is no other foundation to build on! "For no one can lay any foundation other than the one already laid, which is Jesus Christ." (1 Cor. 3:11, WEB)

John confirms this in his first letter, "For there are three who testify: the **Spirit**, the **water**, and the **blood**; and **the three agree as one.**" (1 John 5:7-8, WEB)

The Basics

So, we have established the foundation we build on. Before we can go on from here, we need to make sure we understand the basics, the things any builder has to know before picking up a single power tool. The writer of Hebrews says we move forward when we understand the basics.

> Therefore, leaving the teaching of the first principles of Christ, let's press on to perfection— not laying again a foundation of repentance from dead works, of faith toward God, of the teaching of baptisms, of laying on of hands, of resurrection of the dead, and of eternal judgment. This will we do, if God permits. (Heb. 6:1-3, WEB)

He urges us to move forward to perfection, which is often called "spiritual maturity." God will not permit us to move on in our spiritual development until we master the basics.

So, before we move on let's review the choices we've made and, outline some other things we first need to know, to make sure our foundation is solid.

- **Repentance** — a change of mind which results in a change of action (the working of the word and the Spirit.)

- **Faith in God** — believing in the redemptive work of Jesus (the solid rock of the gospel)
- **Baptism** — a public confession that you have accepted Jesus as your Lord and are repenting of your sin and turning to him. Water baptism is representative of the baptism of the Holy Spirit. God gives you His Spirit, who cleanses you and brings you to life. He enables you to put to death the misdeeds of your flesh and leads you in a new way of life.
- **Resurrection of the dead** — at the end of our lives, God will resurrect the souls of His followers to eternal life, and others to eternal punishment. Later, our bodies will be resurrected and made to last forever (1 Corinthians 15:51).
- **Eternal judgement** — God rewards everyone according to what they have done.

Being grounded in these principles God has laid down for us, we can move on with the construction process.

Sandcastles

I have to admit, I was not a very wise builder in the beginning. And I'm not talking about when I was living in sin, I'm just talking about how I built on the foundation that was laid. As I mentioned earlier, I have experience in construction, and worked doing home improvements like bathroom and kitchen renovations and room additions, and I also worked on some roofing crews. Even though the work was good, I was driven by the American dream. I had a family to provide for, and I wanted the best for my family. There is nothing wrong with wanting the best for your family, but, at that time in my life, I thought that was the end goal. I wasn't really thinking about how to invest my life and family in light of eternity.

I thought if I started my own construction company God would bless it because I was a believer and I was tither (tithing is giving a tenth of your income to the church). Some preach very strongly that if you give financially, you will be blessed financially. God may bless us financially. However, if getting more money is your motive for giving, you may ultimately end up with less! This is true of anything in our lives. When building our lives becomes more important than our spiritual life with God, he may choose to stop the production on the projects that are distracting us.

> *You looked for much, and behold, it came too little*; and when you brought it home, I blew it away. Why? *Because of my house that lies waste, while each of you is busy with his own house.* Therefore, for your sake the heavens withhold the dew, and the earth withholds its fruit.
>
> *I called for a drought* on the land, on the mountains, on the grain, on the new wine, on the oil, on that which the ground produces, on men, on livestock, and on all the labor of the hands. (Haggai 1:9-11, WEB)

I was following the prosperity gospel; I believed being a Christian meant being blessed physically and financially (some call it "health and wealth"). I really was, partially, chasing the money, truth be told. As you can see from Haggai, God warns us against that kind of thinking. Paul says:

> But *those who are determined to be rich fall into a temptation, a snare, and many foolish and harmful lusts, such as drown men in ruin and destruction.* For the love of money is a root of all kinds of evil. Some have been *led* astray from the faith in their greed and have pierced themselves through with many sorrows. (1 Tim. 6:9, WEB)

I was not being led astray from my *faith*, but I was being led astray from my *calling*. I was building on the temporal things of my life, not on the eternal things of my life. I continued to be a witness during this time, serving and sowing financially into the kingdom. I thought that after I made enough money, I would go into full time ministry. I reasoned that I would be a "free agent," with the right financial reserves, and could do everything pro bono, and I wouldn't need to ask anyone for money to support me in ministry. I thought that living that life would show that I was *so* blessed, that I must be living the right kind of godly lifestyle.

In truth, it was a miserable journey! I was always racing the clock, trying to squeeze every dollar out of every minute. Since construction work wasn't really my passion, the work was not enjoyable unless I could see a profit — how pathetic! I've heard it said, "If you can do what you love, you will never work another day in your life." It was another part of my life where I was like a sea turtle stuck in a whirlpool, in the *water*, but missing out on the *ocean*. If the sea turtles don't make it to the open water they were destined for, it makes for a miserable existence! We can expect the same for us if we are not doing what we're *created* and *called* to do for the kingdom. If we aren't following our God-given passion, everything becomes routine and mundane, and there is no life in it.

We are called to advance the kingdom on Earth, not get caught up in the expectations of the earth! When you have a passion and a gift, you want to use it. Passions, gifts, and talents are different for everything, but I knew had been given a passion to preach. During this "prosperity gospel" phase of my life, I will admit I was not mature enough to operate in my calling. I lacked the character that matched the call. I'm thankful, now, that I wasn't preaching at the time, because I have seen so many people promoted in positions of authority and ministry who did not have the character to support them — it has always ended in disaster. I knew I was not ready for public ministry yet, because I had a lot of things to work through, but I did witness whenever I had a chance. Ministry was in my blood; I would even try and turn a job site into a revival service!

The seeds of my passion began being planted in this phase of my life. Looking back, I realize I missed some ministry opportunities because I didn't know how to pursue my calling and I had so much baggage from my past. I did not know anything about spiritual warfare, or how to find my place in the body of believers — it was a rough start. I had a few people come and go that served as mentors, giving me direction, but the rest of my growth came from hard lessons. However, God had a plan, like I said: God doesn't always laugh when we tell him our plans, but when God tells us His plans, we laugh, because it generally does not make sense to our flesh.

"For my thoughts are not your thoughts, neither are your ways my ways, saith the LORD. For as the heavens are higher than the earth, so are my ways higher than your ways, and my thoughts than your thoughts." (Isaiah 55:8-9, WEB)

I continued to struggle along with my construction business. I had a small crew, and we were building condominiums and doing home renovations. At the same time, I was also building debt. I kept spending and charging for home improvements on my own home and projects, thinking I would eventually make enough to pay it all off, at that moment of "big blessing" I was sure was coming. In 2008, it all came crashing down; in the end - *that was the blessing!* Everything I had built was washed away in an instant! I realized very quickly that I had been building castles in the sand.

2008 boasted the biggest single-day market drop in capitalist history up to that point. The housing market crashed; so many were foreclosing on their homes or losing their homes. The home renovations and new construction projects came to a screeching halt in my area. I lost it all! Everything I built was disintegrating right before my eyes. I had told my wife that I had been chasing the wrong dream and that I was tired of riding a dead horse! I had to start all over, again, including finding a new career.

I had a passion for ministry, but I did not know how to get plugged in. I thought I might start by looking for a job working with men who had faced some of the same struggles I had as a younger man. I thought I would pursue becoming a probation officer. I started down the career path, which led me to a job with the Department of Corrections. I truly felt I was seeking God all the way; I could write another book on all the things God did while I was there. However, after serving for almost 5 years, it was time for another change. God began to show me it was time for me move into my passion and calling. It wasn't long after that I had career in full-time ministry. Listen to the words of Paul on how we are to build upon our foundation:

> But if anyone builds on the foundation with gold, silver, costly stones, wood, hay, or stubble, each man's *work will be revealed.* For the Day will declare it, because it is revealed in fire; and the fire itself will test what sort of work each man's work is. If any man's work remains which he built on it, he will receive a reward. If any man's work is burned, he will suffer loss, but he himself will be saved, but as through fire. (1 Cor. 3:12-15, WEB)

I had definitely been using wood hay and straw to build my spiritual house, because I did not have my eternal house in mind when I was in the construction business. It's not that heaven was not on my mind, but I was failing to understand my need to build my house in heaven while I'm here on Earth.

I was going to heaven, and I was building on the foundation, but I wasn't using the right materials for my eternal dwelling. My materials were weak and would not withstand the test of time. I would escape the condemning fire of Judgment Day but would experience loss and frustration. Where we will spend eternity depends on our belief in Jesus. How we will live in eternity depends on how we served Him in this life. We have to keep the final judgment in front of us; our eternal life does not begin with our Earthly death, but it begins at the moment of our salvation. I saw the two as separated, so I focused on building a business, not on building the Kingdom. Our Earthly work, in the name of the Kingdom, will be rewarded.

Stone Castles

Let's look at how to build a solid structure that will survive the test in this life, and in the life to come. Paul describes the building materials at our disposal as, "gold, silver, costly stones," and "wood, hay, or stubble [straw]." Notice there are two different types of materials. One set of materials is combustible and easily consumed by fire. The other type cannot be burned up by fire (melted, yes, but not destroyed). Those materials represent two types of works. Many don't understand that God has "works" for us to do; their faith begins and ends with the correct foundation. They believe, and that is all. I would say most professing Christians have a general knowledge of salvation and the forgiveness of sins, but they don't go much deeper.

God commands more from us. Read what Paul wrote, "For we are His workmanship, created in Christ Jesus for *good works*, which God prepared beforehand that we should walk in them" (Ephesians 2:10, WEB). God has work for us to do; there are *good works* that bring a reward, while other works will result in no reward. Building a castle of stone could be seen as a course in "Good Works 101."

For starters, we are going to look at the two types of works. The Bible says there are dead works and good works. God describes dead works, the things we do outside of His power, this way.

> "But we are all as an unclean thing, and *all our righteousnesses* [works] *are as filthy rags*; and we all do fade as a leaf; and our iniquities, like the wind, have taken us away." (Isaiah 64:6, KJV emphasis mine)

Dead works are of no value before God because they are the kind of works we either did before salvation, or under our own power to impress God. Works like church attendance, tithing, or charitable deeds done while also living in sin are worthless because we cannot *work* our way into a right standing with a holy God. Only God can make us worthy, and He does this by His grace, not our works.

> "How much more shall the blood of Christ, who through the eternal Spirit offered himself without spot to God, purge your conscience from *dead works* to serve the living God?" (Hebrews 9:14, WEB)

God has delivered us from the task of trying to *work* our way back to Him, but that does not mean that God does not have work for us to do. Sometimes, Christians categorize dead works and good works as the same thing, saying, *"all our works like filthy rags,"* and that is not the case. Only dead works stink in the nostrils of God; dead works are comprised of you trying to impress God through human effort. But God created us to *serve* Him through our good works. What are the "good works?" It could be summed up by saying it's "giving your whole life back to God." Helping those in need, being in prayer, being involved in your community, taking care of your family, preaching, teaching, and serving — these and more make up the list of good works we can do when our heart and mind are focused on serving God. The list is endless!

Paul says in his letter to Rome, "Therefore, I urge you, brothers, by the mercies of God, to present *your bodies as a living sacrifice*, holy, acceptable to God, which is your spiritual service" (Romans 12:1, WEB). Since God gave us new lives, we are to live our new lives in service to Him by living the way Jesus lived (1 John 2:6). The outward appearance of good works that serve God is not enough; there is a catch, and it's all about our heavenly reward. It boils down to **who** is doing the good work and for **what** purpose. The Pharisees in Jesus' day would pray, tithe and preach, but only to appear spiritual; those are dead works. Jesus said they have *received their reward*. They wanted the praise of men more than they wanted to please and serve God. As a result, they got what they wanted on Earth, but were given no promise of a reward in heaven.

"Be careful that you don't do your charitable giving [good works] before men, to be seen by them, or else you have *no reward* from your Father who is in heaven" (Matthew 6:1, WEB, emphasis mine). If what I'm doing is just to impress people so they will think I am this spiritual person, then that is my reward. But you can pray, preach, serve, tithe, and *receive a reward* when you're doing it for the glory of God. You have to recognize that it is His Spirit doing the work through you. God does these good works through us, by the grace He has given us. Our good works are for His glory. "Let your light so shine before men, that they may *see your good works*, and glorify your Father which is in heaven" (Matthew 5:16, KJV).

At first glance, those two scriptures from Matthew's gospel may seem like a contradiction. One says, "don't let your works be seen" and the other says do them "so they can be seen." A closer look reveals the key difference: man is glorified in one instance, and God is glorified in the other. It's all about our motive behind our good works *and* our obedience to what He has called and equipped us to do. It's important to know we are NOT saved by works! Jesus did the *work* for our salvation on the cross, through grace. Salvation cannot be earned:

> For it is by grace you have been saved, through faith—and this is not from yourselves, it is the gift of God— *not by works*, so that no one can boast. For we are God's handiwork, *created in Christ Jesus to do good works*, which God prepared in advance for us to do (Ephesians 2:8-10, NIV).

In our salvation, we are re-created in Christ to live like Christ. John Bevere says, "We will not be judged for our sins because Jesus paid the penalty on the cross for our sins." And if we are in Christ our sins are forgiven and forgotten. The scripture we read earlier in 1 Corinthians 3 tells us that our works may be consumed by the fire, but we will still just escape the flames. But who wants to be saved by the skin of their teeth? John also points out the fact that *"we will be judged according to what we were called to do."*

As I said earlier, it's all about our motives behind our good works, *and* our obedience to what God has called and equipped us to do.

Now that we have established the importance of good works vs. dead works, let's take another look at these building materials. The wood, hay and straw are the works I do in the strength of my flesh. For example, if you were *called* to be an accountant, but you *wanted* to be a pastor and you decided to follow your desire, rather than God's purpose by pursuing a career as a pastor, at the judgement everything would be burned up.

Even though you had done the "good work" of full-time ministry, you would not receive a reward because you were doing it for yourself and not for the glory of God. Not only that, but you failed to use the gifts and talents He gave you to do what He called you to do — being an accountant.

Now for the gold, silver and stones which are not consumed. They are the good works that God sees, receives, and rewards. I know a man who had a job with a two-hour commute round-trip. He felt like he was wasting so much time that could be spent reaching people for the kingdom. He said that he remembers crying out to God about it. He went on to say that the Lord said to him, "If I came back tomorrow, and all you had been doing was working this job and providing for your family, I would say, *"well done"*, because you were doing what I wanted you to do at the time." God rewards us according to what He has called us to do!

Now, remember my story? The one about following the Prosperity Gospel. I knew ministry was in my blood after I became a believer. However, I was impatient and wanted to serve God my way, on my timetable. Had I stood before the judgement seat in 2008, everything I built would have been burned up! See, I was not called to build and restore houses (I was for *season*; however, I didn't recognize when it was time to move on). I was called to build and restore lives; those are the works God wanted to do through me. If I had not changed careers, you would not be reading this book. When God is doing the work in us, He is the one who gets the glory. If you stand in a place where you are unsure of your calling, just keep doing the right thing and He will reveal it to you. I've seen Him do this over and over in my life, when I feel stuck, I just keep doing what I know is the right thing, and when the time is completed, God reveals His will. There are things we can do every day that bring glory to God, even when we don't feel we have the direction of a specific calling. How we treat the people we work with, how we serve our employer, how we treat our spouse, children, and neighbors, even how we treat our enemies, these are some of the countless opportunities we have every day to shine God's light and do good works for His glory.

Be encouraged, you may be shining the light of Jesus and not even realizing it. I remember years ago, when I was working at a mission, I saw a man pull into the parking lot driving a van loaded with men who were homeless. He was transporting them from one mission building to another where they served the men food. I will never forget having to take a second look at the driver as he pulled in the parking lot. He had a big smile on his face, and I knew I was looking at Jesus! All I could see at first was the face of Jesus, literally!

I stared intently at the driver; I was finally able to recognize him, but God had allowed me to see the Lord in that man! I was blown away by the smile of God on that man's face as he pulled into the parking lot with those men. Sometimes we think it's the people behind the pulpit, or those writing the big checks, that make God smile, and it's not that we don't need that in the body of believers, but we can never discount the little acts of service that bring God the most joy! Keep serving others in love, for the Bible says,

> "Let's not be weary in doing good, for we will reap in due season, if we don't give up." (Galatians 6:9, WEB)

We close our conversation on the structure and foundation of our lives with this: The fire that will test the quality of our work is the presence and purity of God. If our lives reflect the life of Christ, our work will survive the test. Will we build with the wood, hay and straw, and be consumed, attempting to work for God in our own strength, or will we use the gold, silver and stones that allow God to work through us and receive all the glory? Will your foundation be made of stone (the Gospel of Jesus Christ), cement (the work of the Holy Spirit), and water (The Word), or will it be washed away in the storms like the nests of the sea turtles? You have to choose what you're going to build with.

> If you're wondering how to get the gold, silver and stones from God, all you have to do is *sell your lumber.*

CHARTER GUIDE FOUR
"Castles of Stone or Castles of Sand"

Your fourth choice is to choose your building materials, using either *gold, silver and stones* or *wood, hay and straw.*

- How are you making sure you have a strong foundation made of the Gospel, The Holy Spirit, and the Word?

- Describe a time when you were building sandcastles on the foundation of your life.

- How did those sandcastles affect your life and the lives around you?

- What materials are you using to build your eternal home?

- Has God placed a specific work on your heart for you to do for the kingdom? Describe what it is and how you plan to accomplish what He has called you to do.

- What does it mean to you that we are saved by grace and not by works?

THE CHOICE

You have to choose your materials, either the *gold, silver and stones* or *wood, hay and straw.*

Scripture: But if anyone builds on the foundation with gold, silver, costly stones, wood, hay, or stubble, each man's *work will be revealed.* For the Day will declare it, because it is revealed in fire; and the fire itself will test what sort of work each man's work is.

-1 Corinthians 3:12-13

Thought: Where we will spend eternity depends on our belief in Jesus. How we will live in eternity depends on how we served Him in this life. We have to keep the final judgment in front of us; our eternal life does not begin with our Earthly death, but it begins at the moment of our salvation.

NOTES:

Choice Five

Living Water or Bottled Water

E very living thing needs water for survival. You can survive for over a month without food, but you can't last 3 days without water. If a sea turtle never makes it to the ocean, it will have to search for water in dry places; their entire existence, short and miserable, will be focused on this one task because they were created to consume sea water. A sea turtle trying to survive on land may sound farfetched, but this is exactly what we do as humans. God has an unlimited supply of living water for us, yet we search for water in arid places. There is a story in the Bible where Jesus encounters a woman at a well and has a conversation with her concerning her search for water.

Bottled Water

In John's gospel, he writes that Jesus and his disciples were heading to Galilee, but they *had* to go through Samaria (John 4:4). This was noteworthy because Jews did not associate with Samaritans at all! In fact, they would travel many miles out of their way to avoid even coming near a Samaritan and to make sure they did not set foot on Samaritan soil. Jesus was following the leading of the Spirit, but, because of the custom, it did not make sense to his disciples. This is often the case when God is leading us in a certain direction; in the heat of the moment, it does not make sense to us, or to those around us, but later we see God's reasoning very clearly.

I remember a time I wanted to promote within a company I was working for. I thought this position would create more opportunities, but I did not have peace about it at all. I knew *God* was leading me in a different direction, but I really wanted that position! In fact, I prayed that they would not offer it to me because I didn't know if I would be able to turn it down! Ultimately, they did offer it to me, and I declined (by the grace of God), applying instead for another position that I felt led to take. To make a long story short, I took the second job, the one God wanted me to apply for, and it was amazing the way things turned out! I could write another book on all the miraculous things that took place; in fact, it was from that position that I landed in full-time ministry, serving as one the directors within the organization. If I had taken the other job, it would have been a debacle and I would have missed out on what God was doing in the big picture of my destiny.

So, getting back to the story in John, Jesus is following the leading of the Spirit, and the disciples are perplexed, continuing to follow their Master. As they journey into Samaria, they come to a well just outside of town; Jesus stops, while the disciples continue into town for supplies. At about noon, a Samaritan woman comes to the well for water. This is a very interesting scene, because women generally draw their water in the morning to beat the heat — yet here this woman is coming out at the hottest time of day to draw water! Once she fills her jugs of water, it's possible that the jugs she is carrying may weigh around forty pounds! And she will carry them home, in the desert heat, at the hottest time of day.

Once she arrives Jesus asks her for a drink, because he doesn't have anything to draw water with. She was surprised that He even sparked a conversation with a Samaritan, let alone that He was asking to share her water! She asks Jesus why He is asking her for a drink, and Jesus replies by saying,

> "If you knew the gift of God, and who it is who says to you, 'Give me a drink,' you would have asked him, and he would have given you living water" (John 4:10, NIV).

Jesus goes right to the heart of her circumstances (i.e., her unquenchable thirst); He then reveals to her that He knows she has had several husbands in her life. See, this explains why the woman was coming to the well at the hottest time of day — she was trying to avoid people. Because of her checkered past with men, she is avoiding the other women. In that culture, she would have been looked down upon for having been married so many times. I can only imagine the guilt, shame, and disappointment she was carrying, not to mention all the heartache from each failed marriage. On top of that, she was rejected and was the subject of gossip by the women in the town. Jesus was not there to put her down or to condemn her; in fact, He had gone out of His way, in the desert heat, to meet with her! What He came to do was to set her free from all of that. Like I said, until we are cut deep, we can't see the infection in us. Jesus reveals the woman's infection, that all those men are like bottled waters that she keeps going back for, trying to satisfy her thirst. He cuts her deep by revealing that the only thing that will satisfy her thirst is the living water of His Spirit.

The World is not Enough

We all have had something in our lives that we thought would bring happiness, fulfillment, and satisfaction, only to find ourselves thirsting again. All of us at one time have thought, or maybe you are thinking right now, about something along these lines:

- When I hook up with him, or her, or get married...then I will be happy.
- When I get that promotion...
- Accomplish that goal...
- Finish that project...
- Get that job...
- Start that ministry...
- Lose weight or gain muscle...

There always seems to be something just beyond our reach

that, if we could just get it or achieve it, then we would be satisfied. Here is the deal, though: what we don't realize is that relationships, a goal, ministry, promotion, or whatever that *thing* is, is sometimes in direct competition against God's best for our lives.

Here is something to think about: Jesus asked his disciples, "What will it profit a man if he gains the whole world and forfeits his life (some translations say "soul")? Or what will a man give in exchange for his life?" (Matthew 16:26 WEB). I began to imagine an account balance sheet, but for the world. Then I wondered, what's the bottom line on the entire world's asset section? All the land, buildings, iPhones, iPads, cars, clothing, boats, bikes and mineral rights, all of it! What is the total dollar amount? I Googled it and discovered the value of the world's wealth is currently 431 trillion dollars (roughly).

Let's attempt to put 431 trillion dollars into perspective. Google makes $800,000 per *minute*! Even at that rate, it would take Google 1000+ years to make that much money. Here's a visual example of a trillion dollars: A stack of just *one trillion-dollar* bills would be 67,788 miles high! And just to put a cap on it, if you started counting right now to just *one trillion*, it would take you over 31,000 years.

Having estimated the dollar value of the whole world, my next question is: what would it be like to *gain* the whole world? We only hit on the world's monetary wealth, but what about:

- All the power in the world?
- Or fame?
- Or sex?
- Or servants?

- Or entertainment?
- Or Wisdom?

I began searching for someone who had it all, and what they had to say about it, but no one really seemed suitable. Then it hit me — King Solomon! In his day, he was the wisest, richest, most famous and powerful man in the world. He wrote about the journey he took to find the meaning of life, and what it would be like to have it all and to do it all. He went on this quest because he wanted to know if he could find meaning, fulfillment, purpose, and satisfaction, *apart from God*. And so, he goes for it! He said he had it all: all the money, all the real-estate, all the fame and all the servants (today we call them employees); he also had 300 wives and 700 concubines! Can you imagine that?!?

Then he says,

> "I looked at all the works that my hands had worked, and at the labor that I had labored to do; and behold, all was vanity and a chasing after wind, and there was no profit under the sun" (Ecclesiastes 2:11).

He said it was nothing! Solomon's declaration paints a picture of what Jesus is teaching us in Matthew 16. If you could have it *all* in exchange for your soul — you made a bad deal. You traded the eternal for the temporal. You sold yourself short by underestimating your value. The Bible says God created everything through Jesus, not just our Earth, but all the worlds, galaxies, angels and people (Colossians 1:15-17). How do you put a price on the value of Jesus? It's impossible! Numbers fail; yet

God gave Him up for *you!* So, do not buy the lies that say you're not valuable. *God paid an incalculable price for you!*

The Eternal Thirst

We've all experienced the kind of disappointment that comes from searching to find happiness, fulfillment, and satisfaction in some "one" or some "thing" – only to come up empty. Sometimes, we have to hit rock bottom — run out of bottled water and experience desperate, life-threatening, thirst — before we realize that there is nothing in the material world that can satisfy the thirst for our souls.

There is something I realized that most alcoholics, drug addicts, sex addicts, and others who are enslaved by addictions, have discovered that so many of us miss, and it's this: one is too many, and a thousand is never enough! Now, in light of their revelation, let's look at the words King Solomon wrote concerning the human heart.

He writes,

> "He has made everything beautiful in its time. He has also set *eternity in their hearts*, yet so that man can't find out the work that God has done from the beginning even to the end" (Ecclesiastes 3:11, WEB).

God has placed *eternity* in the heart. There is an *eternal place* in the heart of every man and woman that only the *eternal God* can fill. If you try and fill it with anything else, you will eventually discover it is insufficient. One is too many because the flesh always craves more of something that is pleasing! A thousand won't fill it because the heart that God placed in us is *eternally* vast. There will never be enough money, fame, drugs, sex, or anything else, to fill the eternal place in the heart; only the eternal God can fill the eternal void.

Years ago, I wrote a sermon titled "What's in Your Well?" I came up with the title from my own experiences of trying to satisfy my thirst, which resulted in my digging multiple "wells" to fill my water bottles. For years, I tried to find fulfillment in relationships, accomplishments, money, and position. I would use drugs for every occasion and circumstance, for every problem and pleasure. I was constantly running from one "well" to another. I would travel from city to city, from one relationship to another, and from one job to another. When one "well" was coming up dry, I would run to another to try to satisfy my thirst. I had not yet learned that the peace, joy, and fulfillment that truly satisfies only comes from God.

The Eternal Waters

We return again to Jesus' conversation with the woman at the well. Jesus tells her that He has *living* water for her, and His water will become a spring in her, welling up to eternal life (John 4). This living water in her soul would mean she would no longer have to run everywhere (from man to man, it seemed, in her case) in search of water, because she would have it living within her! That's what our search boils down to: the eternal God *in* us satisfying the eternal thirsts of our souls. We are created by God with the capability to house His Spirit! No other creature on the planet can do that! How amazing, that the Spirit of God, the One who created the universe, can dwell in a human being! If we don't realize that He is all sufficient, that His Spirit in us is what is missing in our lives, then we will go off searching to quench the eternal thirst in the things of this world.

Jesus is recorded later in John's gospel saying,

> "He who believes in me, as the Scripture has said, from *within him* will flow rivers of living water (John 7:38, WEB)."

"From within Him" is referring to the individual who believes. In the Greek "from within" means a hollow space, or cavity, within in the individual — like the stomach of the soul. It is the eternal void that only the eternal God can fill. He fills it with Himself; nothing on Earth can bring true happiness and fulfillment, because things only bring temporary satisfaction. No matter what thing it is you think is quenching your thirst, it's not long before the honeymoon is over, the job becomes work, the drugs wear off, the euphoria dissipates, or the money runs out. The peace and joy that comes from God is not based on external circumstances; it flows from the presence of His eternal Spirit living in us. Sometimes I can actually feel the presence of God, like the joy and peace are filling the stomach of my soul bubbling up.

His Spirit in us produces His nature and character. Paul writes, "But the fruit of the Spirit is love, joy, peace, patience, kindness, goodness, faith, gentleness and self-control. Against such things there is no law" (Galatians 5:22-23, WEB). Jesus said we would know His people by the fruit they bear; the fruit of His people is produced by His Spirit living in us. This Holy Spirit connection is our direct line to God. There are times when I receive a supernatural understanding about something, and I know it came from the Spirit of God in me. I have experienced unexplainable peace when everything around me is falling apart — that's the Spirit of God in me.

It was as Jesus was explaining these living, eternal waters to the woman that she began to feel the conviction of the Spirit about trying to meet her needs in different men. Jesus was being sensitive to this moment of conviction; He did not try and make her feel undeserving, or less than human. Most of the time, when we feel exposed, our first reaction is to run for cover! But the woman at the well is gutting it out. Notice, however, that she does change the subject. She begins to question Jesus about the worship of God.

True Worship

So, the woman spins the conversation, and she begins to question Jesus about where the real place to worship God is. She says, "Our fathers worshiped on this mountain, and you Jews say that in Jerusalem is the place where people ought to worship" (John 4:20, WEB). The Samaritans claimed that the mountain where they worshipped was the right place, and the Jews worshipped in the wrong place. Doesn't that sound so familiar? The Churches today are so divided. One says you can use instruments in worship, and another says no instruments. One says Saturday is the Sabbath day another says Sunday; some will say their church is the only church that will be saved; some argue over baptisms, full submersion or not. I had a friend who was terminally ill and decided to get baptized. However, he was so frail that when they baptized him part of his arm did not go under water and one of his family members insisted that he needed to be baptized again! The man was dying! It was ridiculous! Where does that kind of reasoning end? How long before we have to fly to Israel and be baptized in the Jordan River? In addition to all that, some say you must also speak in tongues. And around and around we go about who is worshipping the "right" way in the "right" place.

Jesus's response is that it's not *where* you worship, it is what's going on inside of you *when* you worship. In light of that definition, let's step back for a moment and ask the question "what is worship?" The word for worship in the Greek is *proskuneo*, it means "to kiss," as in to kiss the hand of a superior. It is commonly associated with bowing down or lying prostrate on the ground, kissing the ground before someone. *Proskuneo* is to show extreme reverence and submission to someone. Today, many sports fans paint a picture of what this worship looks like. Think about the fans who follow their favorite teams (I, too, have my favorites); they wear the jerseys, go to the games and paint their faces. When they are at the games, they are all in! Every fiber of their being is engaged in the game, cheering for their team — that is worship! Jesus is teaching this woman that God wants that kind of sports fan "worship," except He wants it coming from our hearts, not just as pretense. He tells her, "God is spirit, and those who worship him must worship in spirit and truth" (John 4:24, WEB). We are to worship God, from the inside out, in our spirits and in truth, so we have to be honest about ourselves, and honest about who God is. In other words, we have to come clean.

Our problem began with the fall of man; we tend to worship the good things God created, and not God the Creator. Here is something to consider when it comes to worshiping the things in the world verses God. Those teams, players, and all other things we worship, will never give us the time of day. They won't be there cheering for us when we need encouragement. They won't be there when disappointment, heartache, heartbreak and difficulties come. They won't be there to celebrate with us in our victories, but God will! God will always be there. When the storms of life come, He is always ready to help, and He will never miss one of your victories or heartbreaks!

Before Jesus and the Holy Spirit, worship had been very visible and external. However, in this story, Jesus was trying to clue us in on the fact that it's going to become much more internal, because of the Holy Spirit. We still struggle with this idea today.

So many believe church on Sunday is considered "worship," while Monday through Saturday is something separate. But Paul writes that our worship involves every aspect of our lives.

> "Therefore, I urge you, brothers and sisters, in view of God's mercy, *to offer your bodies as a living sacrifice, holy and pleasing to God—this is your true and proper worship.*" (Romans 2:1, NIV).

We must offer ourselves wholly to God for His purposes and plans. Throughout the day, every day, we can offer ourselves in service to God. Doing the dishes, mowing the yard, spending time with family, serving in the community, serving in church, going to work, anything is worship if you have the mindset of giving your whole life to God moment by moment. God doesn't want our worship to feel like a burden. If we are truly filled with His spirit in us, those things can be a joy. Having fun is a part of worship! God is not our Taskmaster. I have been blessed many times out in the ocean as I search for shells, or when I'm fishing, or playing sports. The key to living in an attitude of worship is putting God in the center of everything. Life is so much more enjoyable when you are in relationship with the author of life. This relationship provides you with living water that quenches your eternal thirst, so that you may never need quench your thirst with bottled water again.

CHARTER GUIDE FIVE
"Living Water or Bottled Water"

Your fifth choice is to either drink from God's living water or keep refilling your bottled water.

- Describe a time when you were searching for fulfillment, happiness, or purpose in some "one" or some "thing."

- What has your experience been with feeling like what you had wasn't enough, that you had to continually go back for more to satisfy those desires and longings?

- What does it mean to you that you have access to the free gift of God's Living water, which is His Spirit living in you?

- How has His presence in you affected your life?

- Are you honest with God about yourself?

- Are you living a *life* of worship to God?

THE CHOICE

You have to choose to either drink from the source of *living water* or keep refilling your *bottled water.*

Scripture: "He has made everything beautiful in its time. He has also set *eternity in their hearts,*" -Ecclesiastes 3:11, WEB

Thought: Peace, joy, fulfillment, and all the things that attribute to living life as God would have it are found only in God.

NOTES:

Choice Six

Predestined

P redestination is a churchy word that can be a heated topic. Predestination simply means to determine something in advance. In the context of the Bible, some teach that we are all predestined (or pre-selected) by God for Hell or for Heaven. Others teach that it is a choice for each individual to make whether to believe or not to believe. I believe it is by choice, since the Bible teaches that God wants *all men to be saved.* The apostle Peter writes,

> "The Lord is not slow concerning his promise, as some count slowness; but he is patient with us, *not wishing that anyone should perish*, but *that all* should come to repentance" (2 Peter 2:9, WEB).

I don't think it can get much clearer than that. Jesus died

for the sins of the *whole world,* and He is for *all* people. Now, in light of predestination, the sea turtles paint a picture for us of what it is like to be predestined. Sea turtles are conceived at sea, but they are born on land. But even though they are born on land, they were *created* for the sea; therefore, they are *predestined* to return to the sea, because they were created in the image of their parents. Their destiny can only be found in the ocean they were created for.

Our journey is so similar. In the beginning, Adam and Eve were created in the image of God and walked with God without sin (Genesis 1:27). We are all created in the image of God because we all come from the man and woman, whom God created in His image. Every human being, regardless of race, nationality, gender, or ethnicity, is created in the image of God. We are all born in sin, yet we have been predestined to return to our original state because we are created in His image. Paul writes, "For whom he foreknew, *he also predestined* to be conformed to the image of his Son, that he might be the firstborn among many brothers" (Romans 8:29, WEB).

That is God's plan for us who *choose* to believe. God wants *everyone* to come to a knowledge of the truth. If you don't know the truth about your origins, you won't know what you were created for and who you were created to be. There is so much controversy over a person's identity today because people don't know the truth about who they were created to be, nor do they understand their purpose. We feel like it's impossible to nail down what the truth is for our lives, but that's not because the truth doesn't exist, it's because Satan surrounds the truth with his lies. In fact, the whole purpose of a lie is to hide the truth! Truth is reality while lies are made up!

The Devil keeps us on a rabbit trail in search of the truth. These rabbit trails are what causes all the confusion about who we are as persons, and questions of gender identity and sexual preference. If you can't see the truth about who God created you to be, you will follow the ideas of the world, the flesh and the Devil. "Follow your heart," is an awfully popular phrase, but it is bad advice, because the Bible says,

> "*The heart is deceitful* above all things, and it is exceedingly corrupt. Who can know it?" (Jeremiah 17:9, WEB)

We can be deceived by the desires and impulses of our own hearts! Just because something seems right, or even feels right, does not make it right. This is why we need an objective truth to which we compare our thoughts, feelings and ideas. This kind of truth must guide us without being dictated by emotion or personal preference. This need for truth wasn't part of the original design for you and me, but that it was lost in the fall. Let's go back in time and look at the fall of man, and God's plan to restore man to His original design.

The Fall

In the beginning God put Adam in the garden to work the garden and created Eve as a helper (Genesis. 2:18). God commanded them, saying, "Be fruitful, multiply, fill the earth, and subdue it. Have dominion over the fish of the sea, over the birds of the sky, and over every living thing that moves on the earth" (Genesis 1:28, WEB). That is the first picture of the original design for mankind. He gave us a charge to rule and reign over the earth and to multiply, to have and belong to a family, and to walk with God without being in bondage to sin.

I want to point these things out because the Devil seeks to blind us to the truth about ourselves and who we were created to be; he knows once you get a glimpse of the original design for your life you will realize the one you've been working with (i.e., the worldly design) has been tainted! You can discover who you were created to be by taking the design you have for your life and comparing it to God's original design for your life. That is how you discover the truth about your life; this is another way of filtering out those lies.

Now, the Lord warned Adam that if he ate the fruit from the tree of the knowledge of good and evil, he would die. And this is where the Devil takes the stage, speaking through the serpent:

> Now the *serpent* was more subtle than any animal of the field which God had made. He said to the woman, "*Has God really said*, 'You shall not eat of any tree of the garden'?" The woman said to the serpent, "We may eat fruit from the trees of the garden, but not the fruit of the tree which is in the middle of the garden. God has said, 'You shall not eat of it. You shall not touch it, *lest you die*." (Genesis 3:1-3, WEB)

Eve started out right by reciting the word of God back to

the Devil. However, The serpent said to the woman, 'You won't really die, for God knows that in the day you eat it, *your eyes will be opened*, and you will be like God, *knowing good and evil*' (Genesis 3:4-5, WEB). The Devil's response leads Eve to question the word of God. She knew what the Word said, but she began to entertain the words of the Devil, which is never a good idea. The Devil was planting seeds in the mind of Eve hoping to create a desire within her, which he could then use to manipulate her.

James says,

> "*Evil desires* give birth to *evil actions*. And when sin is fully mature it can murder you! So, my friends, don't be fooled by your own desires (James 1:15-16 TPT)!"

The World English Bible translates it this way: It is their *own heart which is wrong*. That is why he wants to do something wrong. *It fools him*. Then the wrong in his heart makes him do the wrong thing. And the wrong thing he has done leads to death (James 1:15, WEB). Eve had the objective truth of the word of God, but her heart deceived her, and she chose to listen to the Devil. When we question the word of God, it's the first step in the wrong direction. Following the old fishing adage, "hook, line, and sinker" see how the Devil's lies deceived her heart and reeled her in:

When the woman saw that the tree was **good** for food (there is the **hook**), and that it was *a delight to the eyes*, and that the tree was to be desired to *make one wise* (there is the *line*), she took some of its fruit, and ***ate*** (the ***sinker***). (Genesis 3:2-6, WEB, emphasis added)

She also gave some to Adam, and the Bible says, "their eyes were opened" (Genesis 3:7). The knowledge of good and evil infected their conscious minds; it became part of their DNA, and has flowed through every generation, all the way down to ours. In the same way we inherit our parents' physical features, we inherited Adam's sin. Paul said,

> "Therefore, as sin entered into the world through one man, and death through sin; so, death passed to all men, because all sinned." (Romans 5:12, WEB)

After Adam sinned, he became the property of a new master. Paul writes, "Don't you know that when you present yourselves as servants and obey someone, you are the servants of whomever you obey; whether of sin to death, or of obedience to righteousness?" (Romans 6:16, WEB). Jesus tells us we "cannot serve two masters" (Matthew 6:24). Except for Jesus, who was perfect, every person since the fall has lived at least part of their lives under the mastery of sin.

Restored in the Lord

Let's dig a little deeper concerning the creation of man. Personally, I believe it was Jesus who walked with Adam and Eve in the garden, and it was Jesus who created Adam. In fact, Paul says of Jesus:

He is the image of the invisible God, the firstborn of all creation. For by him *all things were created* in the heavens and on the earth, visible things and invisible things, whether thrones or dominions or principalities or powers. *All things have been created through him and for him.* He is before all things, and in him all things are held together (Colossians 1:15-17, WEB).

Because we are created in God's image, we will live forever. The Bible says that God breathed into Adam the breath of life (Genesis 2:7). The Hebrew word for breath is "ruach," it means "breath," "wind," or "spirit," and is used in reference to the Spirit of God. When the LORD breathed into Adam, I believe we get a picture of Adam receiving not only *a* spirit, but the *Holy* Spirit. Here's why I believe that: after Jesus' resurrection, He actually breathes on His disciples and tells them to receive the Holy Spirit (John 20:22). Jesus breathing the Holy Spirit on His disciples paints a picture of man being restored to the original design and brought back into a right relationship with God. We are not just physical beings; we are spiritual beings in a physical body; our spirits return to God for judgment after we die (Hebrews 9:27). Before Adam sinned, his spirit was in perfect fellowship with God's Spirit. When Adam sinned, the union he had with God, through the Spirit of God, was severed. Because of Adam's disobedience, he is now the servant of the Devil.

Without the Spirit of God operating in our lives, we are only flesh and we will gravitate toward the things that satisfy our flesh. That is why it takes conviction to repent, because we don't naturally realize we are spiritually dead and living only to please the desires of our fallen nature. We discussed in Choice Five how we are empty without His Spirit in us. As a result of his disobedience, Adam died to his Spiritual life, but his sinful nature was very much alive! As Paul said, sin came *through* the one man, making us all sinners. When we come into this world, we are totally unaware of the fact that we are missing the Spirit of God in us. The original design for our lives has been tainted and altered by the fall, and that altered design is what we inherit from our earthly parents. But God steps in with His plan to restore our lives. In fact, He had this plan in motion before Eve even took one look at the forbidden fruit! *"For whom he foreknew, he also predestined* to be *conformed to the image of his Son,* that he might be the firstborn among many brothers" (Romans 8:29, WEB). God's plan is to restore us is even better than before! He is not conforming us to the image of Adam, but of Christ!

The Bible says, "Therefore if any man be in Christ, he is a new creature: old things are passed away; behold, all things are become new" (2 Corinthians 5:17, WEB). You are something new! God is re-creating us better than before! I want to add here what Paul said in his letter to Rome, "God has bound all men to disobedience that he might have *mercy on them all"* (Romans 11:32, NIV). Salvation is for *all* because God wants to show mercy to everyone. Paul confirms the free gift of restoration earlier in Romans:

> For if by the trespass of *the one the many died,*
> *much more* did the grace of God, and the gift

by *the grace of the one man, Jesus Christ, abound to the many.* The gift is not as through one who sinned; for the judgment came by one to condemnation, but the free gift came of many trespasses to justification. (Romans 5:15-16, WEB)

Much More Than Before

What Paul is saying there in the sixteenth verse is that even though we are guilty of sinning against God, and deserve condemnation (i.e., death and Hell), the gift of grace we receive in Christ is greater than the condemnation we inherited! Let me put it to you like this: we were all sold as slaves to sin by Adam's disobedience. Since God cannot overlook sin, and because it is part of His character to be just, He must punish sin. The punishment for sin is death because that is what sin does — it kills. So, the question becomes "How can God be in a relationship with mankind, who is bound by sin habitually breaking His laws, and still be a just God?" The answer is this: God sent God the Son, called Jesus (God is one yet He manifests Himself in three persons, Father, Son and Holy Spirit). So, Jesus puts on flesh and is punished in place of man. Just as Adam's *sin* affected all humanity, Jesus was the *sacrifice* for all humanity.

Because Jesus *is* God, His gift of grace for everyone is greater than the trespass of Adam's sin. When you accept God's gift of righteousness, God gives you more grace than you needed when you inherited Adam's sin. God's gift of grace is like an over payment for sin! You will never have any sin in your life that the grace of God cannot cleanse, heal and restore.

> "For if by one man's offense death reigned by one; *much more* they which receive abundance of grace and of the gift of righteousness shall reign in life by one, Jesus Christ." (Romans 5:17, KJV)

Notice the words *"much more."* We have gained "much more" from the Death and resurrection of Jesus than we ever lost to the sin of Adam. Paul reminds us that this is true, "But where sin abounded, grace did *much more* abound" (Romans 5:20, KJV).

Reigning in Life

Not only is His grace more than enough, Paul says we will also *reign* in life! The Greek word for reign is, "basileuo." It means to rule as a king with the implication of complete authority and the right to control without any restrictions! You have *more authority* now in Christ than Adam had in the garden before the fall! Adam had authority over the earth (Genesis 1:28), but listen to how Jesus describes His authority, "Jesus came to them and spoke to them, saying, *'All authority has been given to me in heaven and on earth'* (Matthew 28:18, WEB). He said He has been given "all authority," and we are in Him!

The Lord has been saying these words to me lately, "Everything I am, you are before the Father." I honestly don't even know how to process that statement. But it is found in scripture where John says, "In this, love has been made perfect among us, that we may have boldness in the Day of Judgment, *because as he is, even so we are in this world"* (1 John 4:17, WEB). We are like Him in this world! If we could just get our minds around who we are in Christ, it would be a serious game changer for most of us!

In Christ, you reign over:

- Your flesh and sin.
- The world and its ways.
- The Devil.
- The powers of darkness.
- Your home, or whatever environment you're in.
- Your calling and your service for the Kingdom and the body of believers.
- Every area of Earthly life.

Ultimately, we will reign *with* Him in the eternal kingdom of God. However, you have to choose to receive the life God offers in Christ. In fact, Jesus said, "If you cling to your life, you will lose it, and if you let your life go, you will save it" (Luke 17:33 NLT). What that means is if you try and hold onto what you think your life should be, you will lose your opportunity for eternal life. We have to be willing to die to our old life — the selfish, self-centered, commanding control, perspective of everything in life — and stop refusing to let God in, if we want to receive the true life that He offers us in Christ.

When I think about how the Devil tries to keep us from the truth, I can't help but think of the movie *The Lion King*. In the movie, there is a lion cub named Simba, and he has been predestined to rule and reign as king in the Pride Lands — the kingdom of his father. However, he has an evil uncle named Scar, who covets the throne and plots to get rid of Mufasa (Simba's father) and then kill Simba so that he may become king. To me, that sounds a lot like the Devil who doesn't want us to know that in Christ we are rightfully kings and queens. Jesus said, "The thief only comes to steal, kill, and destroy" (John 10:10, WEB).

The evil uncle Scar succeeds in killing Mufasa, but Simba escapes to a desert where he is rescued by two outcasts. They take him into their home, and he grows up in the oasis with his two new friends. He is taught how to live a carefree life under the motto "Hakuna Matata," which means no worries. While Simba is living a carefree life, his family and friends are all back home suffering under the rule of his wicked uncle, Scar. Simba grows into adulthood under these virtues. My pastor often says, "We don't sin in a vacuum." Everything we do affects the lives of those around us. Later he is discovered by the lioness he was betrothed to as a cub. She insists that Simba return home, confront his uncle and *take his place as king.*

It's not until Simba is confronted by his deceased father's advisor, Rafiki, that he sees the light. Rafiki tells Simba that his father is alive. He takes Simba to a pond and tells him to look into the water. It's there Simba sees the reflection of his father in himself and Rafiki tells him that his father is alive *in him!* I believe the Holy Spirit will lead you to the place where you can see the reflection of the Father *in you!* so He can reveal to you who you were created to be.

In that moment where Simba sees his reflection, the clouds begin to billow and his father appears in the clouds and says to Simba, "You are more than what you have become." Maybe God is telling *you* that. *"You are more than what you have become."* Remember, in Christ, we are "much more than before!" The Devil does not want you to know the power and authority you have in Christ. Simba was able to see the original design for his life — who he was meant to be. He returns home and removes Scar from the throne of the Pride Lands, taking his rightful place as king.

Is that not the gospel?! As believers, we need to see that the Spirit of our heavenly Father lives in us! *We need to de-throne the Devil in our lives and take our rightful place as kings and queens in this life!* Just as the sea turtles were created in, and destined to thrive in the ocean, despite their brief sojourn on land. In the same way, we are created by our God and can only find our rightful place if we return to Him, allowing His Spirit to fill us.

CHARTER GUIDE SIX
"Predestined"

Your sixth choice is to either take your place in the *kingdom of God* or remain a slave in the *kingdom of darkness*.

- How do you view predestination, and why?

- What does it mean to you that you have been predestined to reign in this life?

- What are some ways you can think of that the Devil has deceived you about the truth of who God created you to be?

- How do you see yourself in God's eyes?

- What does it mean to you that God's grace for your life, no matter how many mistakes you have made in the past or will make in the future, not only restores you to a right relationship, but is "even more than before" the fall?

- In Christ you have the grace, power, and authority to rule in every area of your life. Which parts of the world, the flesh and the Devil have you taken authority over? Which ones still need to be surrendered?

THE CHOICE

You have to choose to take your place in the *kingdom of God* or remain a slave in the *kingdom of darkness.*

Scripture: So much more will those who receive the abundance of grace and of the gift of righteousness *reign* in life through the one, Jesus Christ.

-Romans 5:17, WEB

Thought: We have gained "much more" from the Death and resurrection of Jesus than we ever lost to the sin of Adam. Paul reminds us that this is true, "But where sin abounded, grace did *"much more"* abound" (Romans 5:20, KJV).

NOTES:

Choice Seven

The Lost Years

O nce hatchlings make it to the sea, they mysteriously disappear for years. Researchers have struggled to observe where these little hatchlings go during their adolescent years. Similarly, once we are born again into the Kingdom of God, there seems to be a season in the life of many believers where their life in Christ seems out of sight. You may hear believers describe this in hindsight as being in the "wilderness" for a period of time. All throughout the Bible there are accounts of men and woman who faced a wilderness season. The Israelites spent years wandering in the wilderness of the desert. Jacob spent years in a wilderness season, waiting for the wife he was promised. Esther went through a wilderness as an orphan before she was made Queen. Jesus went into the wilderness to be tempted by Satan himself.

Out of all the wilderness stories in the Bible, Joseph, the

son of Jacob, has had the biggest impact on me. No one in the Bible resembles the life of Jesus more than Joseph. He was the favored son of his father. He was betrayed by his brothers. He was sold into slavery, and yet became the deliverer of his people. There is so much we can learn from his "lost years." Let's look at the highlights of his life and how God led him through it all to his, remarkably unfathomable, destiny. We can learn so much from his life regarding how God is able to use all circumstances for His plans and purposes, causing them to work together for our good.

In fact, Paul writes,

> "We know that *all things* work together for good
> for those who love God, for those who are called
> according to his purpose." (Romans 8:28, WEB)

I love how Paul uses the words *"all things."* It assures us that no matter what the circumstances were, or what they are, or what they are going to be, God is God. He says He can make it all work out— just fill in the blank! He is more than able! He has all the power, knowledge, and resources to work *"all things"* together for your good.

The Trials

Joseph's story can be found in Genesis, beginning in chapter 37. In the beginning of his story, we meet a teenager who is immature and somewhat of a tattle tale; he is recorded telling on his brothers for something (the Bible does not say what). He is also a little spoiled; scripture tells us he is his father's favorite, which is symbolized through the gift of a special coat. During this season of his life, God reveals to him that he will one day be in a position of authority, so much so that his entire family would one day kneel before him! Joseph decides to share this revelation with his brothers, and it does not go over well. They were so envious of him that they plotted to kill him. The attitude of the brothers is something we can learn from. When God gives you a dream, vision, or an assignment, not everyone is going to be as excited about it as you are!

Some may even be jealous. You should plan on meeting with some opposition. But don't be discouraged; opposition can be opportunity in disguise.

One thing is evident to me in this season in Joseph's life, and that is that he does not have the character to match the position that he will one day occupy. But also, God knows that; in fact, God is more concerned about our character than our comfort. I've heard it said many times, the only way to develop character is through conflict. Character is the sum total of the mental and moral qualities that distinguish us, and a character that becomes increasingly closer to that of Jesus is vital to our calling and our destiny. Strength of character is what gives stability to a leader.

In the professional world, I have seen so many men and women promoted way beyond their strength of character into positions of authority. My pastor always says, "God will never promote you beyond your character." And he is right, God won't; the problem is, *people* do! I can tell you from experience that it doesn't end well. People get hurt and offended, plus it can take years to recover emotionally and financially as a result of poor leadership. The right leader will have the character to match the power and authority that comes with any position or calling. If you want God to use you in a great way, prepare to suffer greatly! It is the only way to achieve Christ like character.

> Though he (Jesus) was a Son, yet learned
> obedience by the things which he suffered. (Heb.
> 5:8, WEB, parenthesis added)

This is where the character refining process begins for Joseph. One day, he is sent out to check on his older brothers; when they see him coming, they plot to kill him. They seize him, throw him into a pit, and intend to leave him for dead, until one of the brothers decides to sell him to a caravan of slave traders who happened to be in the area. As a result, Joseph is taken to Egypt and sold to a man named Potiphar. So, Joseph has been stripped of everything, sold by his own brothers; he may never see his family or father again. He is in a foreign land with a people who speak a foreign language, act differently and worship differently. I can't even begin to imagine what Joseph was experiencing. However, I will say, that our hardships and wilderness experiences are what prepare and shape us for our destiny.

Joseph's hardships were God's way of preparing him! Although, during the process, Joseph is unaware of why God is allowing these things to happen. So many times, when we are going through a difficult season, or we are in a difficult relationship or career where things seem to be spiraling out of control. We don't understand what is going on and one of the first things we do is begin to question God, wondering where God is. So many times, in these seasons God is moving us closer to what He has called us to do, and the hardships are just preparations for promotion. Joseph cannot see it, but he has just been moved into position! And the Bible says God was with Joseph.

"The LORD was with Joseph, and he was a successful man; and he was in the house of his master the Egyptian. And his master saw that the LORD *was* with him and that the LORD made all he did to prosper in his hand" (Genesis 39:1-3, WEB).

Here is where we have to use caution, because how we respond during these seasons, no matter how long they last, will determine whether or not we're ready to answer the call to promotion. If you give up along the way, amid difficult circumstances, you will not develop the character needed for what God has called you to do.

So, how are we to handle hardships, trials, and mistreatment and so on? James tells us, "Count it all joy, my brothers, when you fall into various temptations, knowing that the testing of your faith produces endurance. Let endurance have its perfect work that you may be perfect and complete, lacking in nothing" (James 2:4, WEB). Honestly, I have yet to meet anyone who was truly excited and joyful about their trials. But what James is saying is that there is a purpose in the midst of the trials we face, and it is in that purpose we find our joy. The United States Marines have a saying, "pain is temporary, but victory is forever." They recognize purpose in the pain!

The pain can have many sources, but we have to face the fact that sometimes the pain comes from the person whose reflection looks back at us from the mirror! I remember when I began to realize I had become the person I hated. I wanted change so badly but didn't know *how* to change. Many of us have spent seasons of different lengths in this type of wilderness. The good news is God knows what it takes to change our character! He knows exactly when, where, how, and how much pain and pressure we must endure to break the mold without damaging the goods.

Our trials refine us, grow us, and temper us. This is crucial not because of our own self-actualization, but because there are lives at stake! Whatever the number is of the people you are able to influence, that is how many you can hurt! As a director in ministry, there have been times I have found myself supervising various operations, with a large number of people to supervise directly, involving numerous businesses, impacting thousands of people throughout the community; everyone involved would either be affected in a positive or negative way, depending on my leadership. We are accountable for the lives and responsibilities God entrusts to us. Jesus said, "To whomever much is given, of him will much be required; and to whom much was entrusted, of him more will be asked" (Luke 12:48, WEB).

Prepared for Promotion

Joseph was being educated during his lost years. He was learning to lead, manage, speak the language of the Egyptians, and conduct business according to Egyptian customs. He also learned how they worshipped and about their social lives. Because Joseph was a Hebrew, there is no way he could have been educated in such affairs had he not been sold into slavery, because the Egyptians would have nothing to do with Hebrews. Some of life's best teachers are our experiences. For about ten years, things went well for Joseph. However, Potiphar's wife had a thing for Joseph, and she had made several attempts to get Joseph to sleep with her. He would not, because of his respect for Potiphar and out of his reverence for God. In a fit of rage, she falsely accuses Joseph of trying to rape her; Potiphar believes her, and has Joseph thrown into prison (Gen. 39). This looks like another huge setback for Joseph, but in reality, he has just been perfectly positioned for God to execute His plan.

If Joseph had given into the temptation of Potiphar's wife, he would have missed the opportunity to be part of the next phase of God's plan. Even though it looks like Joseph was rewarded evil for good, the reality is that God is getting ready to reward Joseph for his faithfulness — through an experience he could only have by being imprisoned! It is time for Joseph to be promoted. He now has the character to match the calling. While Joseph is in prison, God gives him favor with the warden, who puts him in charge of the inmates. One day while Joseph was serving the inmates, he came across two men who were servants of Pharaoh, the king of Egypt. One of them was the cup bearer and the other was the baker. They both had displeased Pharaoh and were put into prison for it. Joseph notices that they seemed troubled about something and inquires them about it. They replied that they both had unsettling dreams, but there is no one who can interpret them. Joseph asked them to explain the dreams to him and he was able to interpret both of them. Here is the account of the dream of **the cup bearer:**

> The chief cup bearer told his dream to Joseph, and said to him, "In my dream, behold, a vine was in front of me, and in the vine were three branches.

It was as though it budded, it blossomed, and its clusters produced ripe grapes. Pharaoh's cup was in my hand; and I took the grapes, and pressed them into Pharaoh's cup, and I gave the cup into Pharaoh's hand."

Joseph said to him, "This is its interpretation: the three branches are three days. Within three more days, Pharaoh will lift up your head, and restore you to your office. You will give Pharaoh's cup into his hand, the way you did when you were his cup bearer. But remember me when it is well with you. (Genesis 40:9-14, WEB)

Then **the baker** tells Joseph his dream:

When the chief baker saw that the interpretation was good, he said to Joseph, "I also was in my dream, and behold, three baskets of white bread were on my head. In the uppermost basket there were all kinds of baked food for Pharaoh, and the birds ate them out of the basket on my head."

Joseph answered, "This is its interpretation. The three baskets are three days. Within three more days, Pharaoh will lift up your head from off you, and will *hang you on a tree*; and the birds will eat your flesh from off you." On the third day, which was Pharaoh's birthday, he made a feast for all his servants, and he lifted up the head of the chief cup bearer and the head of the chief baker among his servants. He restored the chief cup bearer to his position again, and he gave the cup into Pharaoh's hand; but he hanged the chief baker, as Joseph had interpreted to them. Yet the chief cup bearer didn't remember Joseph but forgot him. (Genesis 40:16-23, WEB)

I wanted you to read these verses because they are symbolic for communion. God prepared Joseph for promotion through the same symbols He used to prepare His son to go to the cross at the last supper. God revealed this to me some time ago, just as I was preparing to give a sermon on the life of Joseph. I could see it so clearly: the cup bearer represented the wine, and the baker represented the bread, and both of them were given 3 days, just as Jesus was three days in the grave.

Before this revelation, I had always wondered why the baker had to die; then it became clear that his body had to be broken just like Jesus (Note: Joseph said the baker would *"hang on a tree"*). The cup bearer represents the blood, and he is restored to the palace to speak to the king for Joseph. In the same way, the blood of Jesus speaks to the Father for us — we call this intercession. While Jesus does his job perfectly, the cup bearer forgot all about Joseph for about a year. It wasn't until Pharaoh had two dreams that neither he, nor anyone else in the kingdom, could interpret that the cupbearer remembered Joseph. The cupbearer tells the King about Joseph, how he interpreted his dream in prison. Pharaoh has Joseph summoned to see if he can interpret the dreams. When Joseph appears before Pharaoh, he tells Pharaoh that only God can give the interpretation. I just love that! Joseph is careful to give God the glory, not himself.

He could have used his gift as a bartering chip, but instead he chose to make sure God was the one who was exalted. So, Pharaoh tells Joseph his dreams, and Joseph interprets them. Joseph reveals to Pharaoh that his dreams predict a famine is coming. He will have seven good years to prepare for seven bad years to follow.

Joseph advises him to find someone wise to handle all the preparations. Pharaoh responds:

> Pharaoh said to his servants, "Can we find such a one as this, a man in whom is the Spirit of God?" Pharaoh said to Joseph, "Because God has shown you all of this, there is no one so discreet and wise as you. You shall be over my house. All my people will be ruled according to your word. Only in the throne I will be greater than you. *Pharaoh said to Joseph, "Behold, I have set you over all the land of Egypt."* (Genesis 41:37-41, WEB)

Everything Joseph had gone through led him to this moment. He was second in command of the nation of Egypt. Not long after the good years were gone, Joseph's brothers came to Egypt in search of food; they unknowingly found themselves on their knees before the brother they had betrayed. Joseph, upon revealing who he was, was merciful, and he forgave his brothers and explained that what they meant for evil, God used for good to deliver His people.

Forgiveness Over Bitterness

This is such an important scene in the story because the Bible tells us we are to forgive one another. I have heard preachers say that "Holding on to unforgiveness is like drinking poison and hoping the other person dies." It is toxic for us to hold onto unforgiveness, and it destroys relationships. Imagine if Joseph had allowed bitterness to harden his heart, causing him to withhold forgiveness from his brothers. Instead of the story being about how his brothers nearly killed him, it would be about how Joseph was placed in a position to save his brothers but chose to condemn them. You see, It's not the offense that destroys a relationship, because it is inevitable that we are going to offend or hurt someone, whether intentionally or accidentally, but it is the unwillingness to forgive that destroys relationships.

Here is an example of how refusing to forgive destroys relationships. As a child, I was very impatient, *(I'm still working on it),* and I remember a time in the first grade when our class was at recess and several of us were taking turns crossing the monkey bars. The kid in front of me was taking so long to swing from one to the other that I decided to take off swinging my way to the other side. Now, there was only room for one person to swing across at a time, and when I caught up with the kid in front of me, I was not able to swing around him and I ended up knocking him off the bars — that part was an accident. Nonetheless, when he fell, he landed on his arm and it broke! I remember sometime later we were on the school bus, and I realized I had never apologized to him. I saw there was a seat open by him, so I sat down and told him how sorry

I was for the time I accidentally broke his arm. He said if it happened again, he would beat me up! He was unwilling to forgive! There is no way to restore a relationship if someone is unwilling to forgive. The person who won't forgive becomes the Devil's property. Jesus said, "But if you don't forgive men their trespasses, neither will your Father forgive your trespasses" (Matthew 6:15, WEB).

When I think of how we are taken captive by holding on to unforgiveness, I'm reminded of a video I saw on how certain natives capture monkeys. They cut a small hole in a melon or something like it, just big enough for a monkey to put his hand in and they bury it in the ground. They then put a banana in the buried melon and wait for the monkey to reach in for it. Now, once the monkey gets a hold of the banana, he will not be able to get his hand out of the melon. As long as he is holding onto the banana, he cannot get free, because the opening is too small for his hand and the banana together. The only way for the monkey to get free, is to let go of the banana. Satan baits us in the same way. He uses the offenses of others as bait to keep us in bondage, and the only way to get free is to let go of the offenses and forgive. We do not forgive to let *others* off the hook, we forgive to let *ourselves* off the hook! Unforgiveness breeds bitterness and does not build the strength of our character. Paul tells us, "And be kind to one another, tender hearted, forgiving each other, *just as God also in Christ forgave you*" (Ephesians 4:32, WEB).

I've heard it said, *"We are never more like God than when we forgive."* Joseph was clearly acting like God when he forgave his brothers. Joseph grew in strength of character, from an entitled, self-important teenager, to a servant, to a prisoner, to chief advisor to Pharaoh.

God promoted Joseph, after he had grown into his calling as a result of those lost years. After Joseph forgave his brothers, he had his entire family moved to where he was, and he made sure they had all they needed from the stores Egypt had prepared. This is a beautiful picture of how Jesus forgives all of us and wants us to be with Him in His kingdom forever. He does not only forgive us, but He gives us out of His abundance. Joseph's story encourages us to persevere, because no matter what we are going through, what we have done, or what has been done to us, God is able to use it *all* for our good and His glory.

CHARTER GUIDE SEVEN
"The Lost Years"

Your seventh choice is to either persevere or remain bitter.

- What times in your past can you now see as seasons when God was using adversity to mold you and prepare you for something in the future?

- What trials are you facing now?

- How are you responding in your trials?

- Is there any unforgiveness in your relationships that is affecting your ability to persevere?

- What does it mean to you that God can work all things together for your good?

- How do you see yourself conforming more and more to the image of His Son?

THE CHOICE

You have to choose *to persevere* through your lost years, the years of preparation, knowing that when the time is just right, your promotion comes; or you can choose *to remain bitter,* going nowhere, feeling sorry for yourself.

Scripture: "We know that *all things* work together for good for those who love God, for those who are called according to his purpose" (Romans 8:28, WEB).

Thought: Through our hardships God is moving us closer to what He has called us to do, and the wilderness seasons are the preparations for promotion.

NOTES:

Choice Eight

Armed or Endangered

A sea turtle has only two primary things to defend itself with, its mouth and its shell. A sea turtle's shell can withstand thousands of pounds of pressure, this shell functions as a suit of armor against the predators in the sea. Even though we are in God, and His Spirit is in us, we still face the threat of predators. We live in a fallen world with fallen angels and fallen people. There is a battle being waged between the Kingdom of Darkness and the Kingdom of Light and we need to be armed and aware of our enemy.

The Unseen Enemy

A year or so after I became a Christian, I was seriously seeking a deeper walk with God after living in the shallows. Once I got serious, so did the Devil! One night, I awoke from my sleep hearing a voice threatening me; I could not see anyone, and I could not move either! I was completely paralyzed! All I could do was lay there and listen to this demon tell me how he was going to kill me. I kept thinking, "If I could just get the name of Jesus out of my mouth this would stop." This went on for a few minutes until, finally, I could speak, and the first word out of my mouth was Jesus! It was *over* after that. I don't share that experience very often, but about 12 years after this happened, I was out of town on business for our company with one of my co-workers. We were both Christians, and I don't remember exactly what started the conversation, but he began talking about spiritual warfare and went on to tell me about a time in his life when he was awakened in the night and could not move! He had the exact experience as I did! I'm sure Satan would love for us to think we are crazy, so that we just keep these experiences to ourselves.

The closer we move toward the call of God and the more we seek to press into God, the more present and active the enemy becomes! I've heard preachers say, *"For every new level there is a new Devil waiting."* If he can't take you to Hell for eternity, he will do everything he can to bring it to you here on Earth! He will battle you in your job, in your marriage, with your children, in your ministry, and most definitely in your mind! In fact, the battlefield at large is in your mind. He will attack your thoughts to gain control of your emotions and actions. As a believer, your battle is against the kingdom of darkness and the spiritual powers in the unseen realm. The Apostle Paul endured many battles, and he wrote to us, saying, "For our wrestling is not against *flesh* and *blood*, but against the principalities, against the powers, against the world's rulers of the darkness of this age, and against the spiritual forces of wickedness in *the heavenly places*" (Ephesians 6:10-12, WEB).

After studying this for years I came to the conclusion that Paul was making it a point to tell us that we are not fighting *flesh* and *blood*.

So many times, we think our fight is with:

- Our boss.
- Our co-worker.
- Our spouse.
- Our children.
- Our government.
- Our addictions.
- Our identity.
- Our sexuality.
- Our gender.
- Our lust.
- Our bad attitudes.

What Paul is saying, however, is that while the enemy can work *through* those feelings and people, they are not the enemy. We need to protect, and pray for, the people we love and be sensitive to the fact that the enemy may have gained a foothold in their lives and is therefore trying to use them as instruments of destruction in our relationships. We also need to be aware that he is using the desires of our fallen nature to arouse, confuse, and misdirect our emotions and desires.

I will admit, at times I forget we are in a battle. As a result, I'm not always as prepared as I should be when the attacks come. I've been blindsided so many times, in places like my marriage and my job, because I failed to realize it was the enemy working through somebody. Don't neglect something else we need to watch out for: *sometimes we are the ones the enemy is working through!* We don't like to think about, or admit, that the enemy could have this power over us, so we have to be honest about the frailty of our own nature. There will be times when you will blow it, no matter how mature you are — it's just reality! It's a major advantage the enemy has on us that we cannot always see or recognize him.

Know Your Enemy

Our enemy, the Devil, is described as a predator. "Be sober and self-controlled. Be watchful. Your adversary, the devil, walks around like a roaring lion, seeking whom he may devour" (1 Peter 5:8, WEB). Predators detect vulnerabilities in their prey; they go after the weak, the young, the sick, and the injured. They follow the scent of suffering and then make their move. The enemy who fights to thwart your purpose and destiny hunts with that same killer instinct, with a cold-hearted and ruthless hunger, just waiting for the right moment to attack its prey.

There are more than likely billions of fallen angels working to destroy mankind, and they have been hunting game for centuries. Your enemy takes the time to study you, and more than likely he has been working in your family for centuries. I believe demons work from generation to generation. Think about how often we see those who struggle with drugs and alcohol pass it down to the next generation. Those who thirst for money and power pass it down. Sexual addictions are passed down. Look at how addictions, behaviors, habits and hang-ups are passed down from generation to generation! From the time you took your first breath, the enemy of your soul has been studying you, your family, and everyone connected to you. He knows your strengths, weaknesses, triggers, habits, likes, and dislikes. He more than likely knows you better than you know yourself. This is why it is crucial that you know who you are in Christ!

A Child of God

In the Apostle Paul's letter to the Ephesians, he spends time reminding the believers who they are in Christ and the blessings and power that are available to them. I remember years ago going with some friends to see the new Spiderman movie. The special effects and graphics were awesome, and I remember feeling stirred in my spirit as I watched Peter Parker transform into Spiderman. I felt like I was getting a revelation. I remember noticing how at first, he had no idea that he had been changed and no concept of the power with which he had been endowed. He did not know that when he was bit by this unique and rare Spider that it actually changed his DNA. The spider bite had literally changed him into a new species. He had powers and abilities he never had before. While all this was all unfolding, God was showing me that, in Christ, we have been endowed with power and special abilities we never had before — like Spiderman! We are literally new creatures in Christ. Scripture says, "Therefore if any man be in Christ, he is a *new creature*: old things are passed away; behold, all things are become new" (2 Corinthians 5:17, WEB).

Being a new creature, of a new species, means your DNA has been changed! You are no longer the person you were. We have new desires, new thoughts, new ways, new works, and a new understanding of the things of God. We possess new abilities and spiritual gifts that we didn't have before. You're now a child of God, with angels watching over you and the Holy Spirit living in you. You have been changed; you now have authority over the Devil. He is aware of this transformation, and he does not want you to know who you are and what is available to you through the One who is living in you. When I started learning these things about my spiritual life, and the authority I have in Christ over my enemy, it was a real game changer! I realized that I'm no longer bound by my carnal cravings. I began to realize how much the Devil influences those desires. When I realized that I'm not wrestling with lust, or an addiction, or a bad attitude but that I'm really wrestling with spiritual forces, I began to gain the victory in so many areas of my life. I gained the victory over my addictions, lusts, and habits — my whole life began to change in every area. I received victory because I was aware of the armor that was available to protect me. If you want the victory, you must go into battle wearing the armor God has provided for you.

The Armor of God

Paul writes, "Finally, be strong in the Lord, and in the strength of his might. Put on the whole *armor of God* that you may be able to stand against the wiles of the devil" (Ephesians 6:10, WEB). The reason for this special armor is because we don't fight the way the world fights; we do not use the weapons of the world for our warfare.

Paul confirms this in his letter to Corinth:

> "For though we walk in the flesh, *we don't wage war according to the flesh*; for the weapons of our warfare are not of the flesh, but mighty before God to the throwing down of strongholds" (2 Corinthians 10:4, WEB).

We don't use our hands, or other worldly weapons, in battle, because our battles are spiritual battles. Just like the sea turtles, our line of defense is the armor that God has provided for us; the apostle Paul refers to it as the armor of God. Think about it — this is *God's* armor! Nothing gets through God's armor! Being strong in the Lord means we choose to rely on His power in us. The prophet Isaiah says:

> "No weapon that is formed against you will succeed; and every tongue that rises against you in judgment you will condemn. This [peace, righteousness, security, and triumph over opposition] is the heritage of the servants of the Lord, and *this is* their vindication from Me," says the Lord. (Isaiah 54:17, AMP)

God has already promised His children the victory! We just have to put on His armor. I studied martial arts for a few years, and I can tell you there is a big difference between being in a fight *with* protective gear and *without* it; without armor, there is a lot more bloodshed! Without the armor, we run the risk of becoming an endangered species, which is exactly what the enemy wants! He does not want you and I armed when we go into battle, and he certainly doesn't want multiple believers standing together as an army against the enemy.

Let's look at the armor and how to use it in battle:

> Therefore, put on the whole armor of God that you may be able to withstand in the evil day, and having done all, to stand. **Stand therefore**, having the utility **belt of truth** buckled around your waist, and having put on the **breastplate of righteousness**, and having fitted **your feet with the preparation of the Good News of peace**, above all, taking up the **shield of faith**, with which you will be able to quench all the fiery darts of the evil one. And take the **helmet of salvation**, and the *sword of the Spirit*, which is the word of God; with all prayer and requests, **praying at all times in the Spirit**, and being watchful to this end in all perseverance and requests for all the saints. (Ephesians 6:13-18, WEB)

Stand Firm

I have highlighted 7 things described in this passage from Ephesians. The first is **stand**. Like I said, I have a background in martial arts. Years ago, I met an instructor who had several black belts in various styles, and he was teaching a technique I had never heard of, so I decided to take a class. The style of fighting was very unique; it was mainly focused on how people stand and position themselves in a fight or in battle. There is a mechanical technique that can be applied based on how someone is standing. There is a triangle that can be seen in every stance if you know how to look for it, and when you find it, you know that is the weakest point in the stance.

I was teaching a group of men about the armor of God in a service one night, and I asked, "Who is the biggest man in the room?" We identified him and I had him come forward. He was bigger than I expected, and at the time I weighed about 170 pounds. This guy had at least a hundred pounds on me, not to mention he was much taller than I was! I proceeded to demonstrate how vulnerable we can be in our stance; I executed the triangle technique on the volunteer from the audience and down he went! The men were all surprised, and so was I! (I will admit, I was a little nervous.)

The enemy is the same way. He looks for those weaknesses in our stance. You have to be confident you're in right standing with God when the enemy tries to condemn you. You have to know you have authority over the enemy. You have to stand firm in your convictions. Your posture alone speaks volumes to the adversary. So, stand firm; stand in power, and in the authority God has given you, and remind yourself you are a child of almighty God!

The Belt of Truth

Next comes the belt of truth. The number one thing the enemy uses is deception; it is the deadliest thing on Earth! When you're deceived, you are convinced you are right when in fact you are dead wrong! _Literally_, I've seen people, including myself, almost die from falling victim to deception! That's why we need the objective truth of Scripture as a reference point. We cannot even trust our own thoughts at times. I mentioned it earlier in the book, but I want to show you again; the Bible says, "The heart is deceitful above all things and beyond cure. Who can understand it (Jeremiah 17:9, WEB)?" We have to compare our own thoughts, and guidance from others, against the word of God to avoid being deceived.

King David prayed,

> "Search me, O God, and know my heart: try me, and know my thoughts: And see if there be any wicked way in me and lead me in the way everlasting" (Psalm 139:23-24, WEB).

We do not always know what is lurking in our own hearts; that is why we need the word of God to read us. The Bible will actually read us if we let it. The word of God is alive, and it can reveal your real motives behind every decision, which can sometimes be painful. You may have to give up a relationship, or stop participating in a certain activity, or whatever the Word reveals. It will be a sacrifice, but it will also spare you future heartaches, and may even save your life. The truth protects us against deception.

The Breastplate of Righteousness

One night I was awakened with the thought of these words, "pursue righteousness." For years, I focused on my righteousness and what my part was in maintaining a right standing with God. After that word was planted in my mind, I prayed about it and realized it was a word from the Lord. So, I began studying righteousness; you could say I went on a quest. In fact, Jesus said, "But seek first God's Kingdom and *his righteousness*" (Matthew 6:33, WEB). About a year later, I began to understand it was *His* righteousness I needed. God has made us right with Himself! It wasn't anything I did, it was what Jesus did that makes us right with God. Remember when I said I heard the Lord whisper to me, "Everything I am you are before the Father." That, to me, is still mind blowing. Everything He is, we are before God. Think about Jesus' right standing with God, His holiness, His authority, His sinlessness before God; since Jesus is God's Son, and we are like Jesus, that makes us all sons and daughters of the Father.

We have to know that we are standing in right standing with God. The breastplate of a soldier protects the most vital organ in the body which is your heart. Righteousness is the breastplate because you have to know you are righteous, or you're dead! The Devil will work you to death by making you think you are not righteous until you start performing on a certain level. Listen: *everything we do flows from the grace, mercy, and love God has for us!* That is where we start! That is the foundation of everything. We discussed this earlier, we don't *build* the rock; we build *on* the rock!

God made the first move; we were dead in sin when He called us, and He made us right. Paul writes,

> "But God, being rich in mercy, for his great love
> with which he loved us, even when we were dead

through our trespasses, made us alive together with Christ—by grace you have been saved." (Ephesians 2:4-5, WEB)

God made us right with Himself, and He provides us with everything we need to live righteously before Him; that is how it works. After about a year of studying this, my wife and I were in South Carolina visiting our daughter. We decided on the way back we would go through North Carolina so we could visit the Billy Graham library. When we arrived at the library, there was a path just off to the side of the library which led to Ruth Graham's gravestone. On the stone, something was written in Chinese, but it did not translate the writing anywhere on the stone. We then went inside and toured the library, and at the end of the tour we went into the gift shop. While I was looking around, I saw a necklace with the same marking that was on Ruth's stone, so I asked one of the clerks what it meant. The clerk replied, "Righteousness." I knew then that my quest was over because I understood what the Lord was teaching me about His righteousness.

The Shoes of Peace

Paul says, "having fitted your feet with the preparation of the Good News of peace" (vs.15). We are to walk with the readiness of the gospel. In fact, God says,

"How beautiful on the mountains *are the feet* of him who brings good news, who publishes peace, who brings good news, who proclaims salvation, who says to Zion, 'Your God reigns (Isaiah 52:7, WEB)!'"

We are to walk in peace and share the good news. We can do that simply by the way we carry ourselves. Are you quick to judge, harsh, hard to get along with and easily offended, or are you quick to forgive, even your enemies? We need to be eager and ready to do good, not only *bringing* the message of peace, but actually *being* the message of peace that people can see in our lives.

There have been many times in my life where I have had conflicts with co-workers, and I started handling it the same way each time. No matter who was at fault, whether it was my own stupidity or not, what I started doing was giving gifts to the person I was having issues with. I would buy them a gift card to a restaurant, or something else I knew they were interested in. Paul writes, "Don't be overcome by evil, but overcome evil with good" (Romans 12:21, WEB). I did something good in these situations, bringing literal "peace offerings." By finding ways to keep peace with others, even when there is tension, we keep the enemy from infecting us with unforgiveness, bitterness, and other toxic emotions.

The Helmet of Salvation

You have to protect your head from the lies of the enemy. The protection has to be impenetrable. The safety of your head has to be certain in physical battle in the same way the safety of your mind has to be protected in spiritual battle. Are you saved? Do you have the assurance of salvation? Because condemnation is another big deception the enemy loves to use. He will condemn you for your past sins and shortcomings; he'll throw every mistake and wrong thing he can conjure up at you. In Revelation, it says,

> I heard a loud voice in heaven, saying, "Now the salvation, the power, and the Kingdom of our God, and the authority of his Christ has come; for the accuser of our brothers has been thrown down, *who accuses them before our God day and night.* They overcame him because of the Lamb's blood, and because of the word of their testimony. They didn't love their life, even to death." (Revelation 12:9-11, WEB)

He is the deceiver of the whole world, and he is down here *accusing us day and night!* He is busy pointing the finger at you! That is why you have to know who you are in Christ and that you are saved by the blood of Jesus.

But don't miss the victory in those verses! We overcome him by the blood. The word overcome in the Greek can also mean to *conquer.* The enemy has been totally defeated by Jesus on the cross, God has "paid in full" for your redemption! The Devil has no legal right to you because God has paid the price for your sins, your freedom, your salvation, and for your healing. In fact, every promise God has made in the Bible is yours through the blood of Jesus! We are more than conquerors (Romans 8:37)! We have complete victory over the enemy; fortify your mind with the full understanding of your salvation.

The Sword of the Spirit

The sea turtles have one other weapon of defense, their mouth. We use our mouths to wield the sword of the Spirit — the word of God. All scripture is God breathed. The Bible is the most unique book on the planet. There has never been anything written like it; it is alive with the authority of God. We have to use the Word against the enemy.

When Jesus was in the desert 40 days, being tempted by the Devil, He fought back using the Word. Sometimes we have to get vocal with the enemy. I admit, I am not always quick to use scripture when the enemy is attacking my mind. Even while I was writing this book, I started feeling depressed, oppressed, and discouraged; my wife thought I needed to talk with a counselor. But I realized that the things that were going through my mind were of the Devil. I remember sitting in my car, and I had just had enough of it. I verbally rebuked the Devil! And those negative feelings and thoughts left me instantly! I felt like the Lord said to me "It's about time!" And it was about time that I wielded the greatest weapon at my disposal. We have to equip the sword in battle; it won't do any good sitting on a shelf or memorized in our hearts and minds if we are not going to apply it to our lives and use it against the enemy.

Prayer in the Spirit

Praying in the Spirit is a powerful thing. We read in the book of James, "The heartfelt *and* persistent prayer of a righteous man (believer) can accomplish much [when put into action and made effective by God—it is dynamic and can have tremendous power]" (James 5:16, AMP). I will never forget the time I was standing in my living room, and I was praying passionately for a friend. I just felt moved to pray for him, and as I prayed, it was like there was an amplifier in the room; it was like praying under an open heaven. At this time, he was away from the Lord. Two days after I prayed, I received a phone call from him. He began to tell me about how he almost drank himself to death. He went on to say that he actually passed out and he said he remembers everything going dark and that he could see a small light in the distance coming at him. He said it kept getting closer and closer until he could see it was the figure of a man as the light continued coming toward him.

My friend then realized it was the Lord! He said he looked into His eyes and His pupils looked like they had stars inside of them; he said it was an amazing sight. He said the Lord put His hand on his shoulder and said, "I want to help," and then he woke up. He said when he woke up, he could still feel the Lord's hand on his shoulder! I asked, "When did all this happen?" and he said, "Two days ago." I was beside myself! I told him how two days ago I had been praying for him. There is nothing like the power of prayer in the Spirit!

When we are in Christ, we come armed and equipped with all we need to win the battle against the enemy, as we read in Ephesians 6. But God will not force us to fight. Even with the greatest weapons and protection at our disposal, we can, and often do, fail to use them effectively. Much like the shell of a sea turtle can endure immense pressure, the armor of God can withstand anything you throw at it. If sea turtles didn't have this built-in protection, they would certainly become endangered at the hands of the many predators in the sea, if not extinct! In making sure that we use the power and protection of God to the fullest against the enemy, we assure that our species is not only protected from being endangered, but is thriving.

CHARTER GUIDE EIGHT
"Armed or Endangered"

Your *eighth choice* is to be *armed* or *endangered*.

- What does it mean to you that you have an enemy you cannot see?

- In what ways have you experienced spiritual warfare?

- How has the enemy worked through flesh and blood to deceive you?

- How are you using God's armor to fight against the enemy?

- What are some ways you can tell you are a new creature in Christ?

- Are you aware of any spiritual gifts you have received?

THE CHOICE

You have to choose to either be *armed* or *endangered.*

Scripture: "For though we walk in the flesh, *we don't wage war according to the flesh*; for the weapons of our warfare are not of the flesh, but mighty before God to the throwing down of strongholds." -2 Corinthians 10:4, WEB

Thought: *"For every new level there is a new Devil waiting."*

NOTES:

Choice Nine

Salt Waters or Fresh Waters

Sea turtles are created for salt water. For them to try and live and survive in a freshwater environment would not be impossible, but it would make life very difficult. Without the assistance of salt water, the sea turtle would struggle to maintain buoyancy, and it would be very difficult to swim away from predators. Sea turtles are also created to consume salt water and to feed on the resources of the sea. A sea turtle out of its natural habit is set up for a very difficult and stressful life. It's not that a sea turtle could not survive at all in fresh water, but why choose to live in an environment that would be more difficult and dangerous? Yet that is exactly what we do when we choose to live a life apart from the grace of God and from the life-giving waters that He desires for our lives.

Swimming Upstream

The Bible says life is hard when we are outside of His salt waters for our lives. Solomon wrote, "Good understanding giveth favor: but the way of transgressors is hard" (Proverbs 13:15, KJV). To be a transgressor is to be outside of the will and precepts of God — to be in sin. When we are outside of God's plan for our lives, we are swimming upstream; everything feels heavy and restrictive. There is no buoyancy in our lives. I lived like that for years! It seemed like everything was a struggle; in my relationships, and at work, I felt like I could not get the victory in life on any level. When we are outside of God's will, when we are dominated by our sinful nature we cannot please God. "For the mind of the flesh is death, but the mind of the Spirit is life and peace; because the mind of the flesh is hostile toward God; for it is not subject to God's law, neither indeed can it be. *Those who are in the flesh can't please God*" (Romans 8:6, WEB).

Life without the Spirit and favor of God is like constantly swimming against the current of our destiny. However, when God is pleased, we experience the power, presence, and providence of God. Isaiah said,

"He will guide you continually, satisfy your soul in dry places, and make your bones strong. You will be like a watered garden, and like a spring of water whose waters don't fail" (Isaiah 58:11, WEB).

That doesn't mean that we won't face difficulties as believers; the difference is that, when you're in the economy of God, there is a flow to your life, you experience blessings and breakthroughs. God opens doors of opportunity that otherwise would have been shut. There is healing for your body, and in your soul; relationships are restored. The stress and strain of doing everything in your own strength is removed once you learn how to flow with the current of God's Spirit. And even when you do encounter difficulties and opposition, you don't experience fear; rather, you experience love and power. "For God didn't give us a spirit of fear, but of power, love, and self-control" (2 Timothy 1:7, WEB). Also, life in the Spirit allows us to trust God, we don't default to taking control when we don't get our way, because we have the Spirit of self-control in our hearts. "If the Spirit of him who raised up Jesus from the dead dwells in you, he who raised up Christ Jesus from the dead will also give life to your mortal bodies through his Spirit who dwells in you" (Romans 8:11, WEB).

God provides all the power we need for life through His Spirit in us. One of the functions of the grace of God in our lives is a supernatural enabling to do what God requires us to do according to His word. Paul said, "God is able to make *all grace abound* to you, that you, always having all sufficiency in everything, may abound to every good work" (2 Corinthians 9:8, WEB). You should highlight "all grace abound," because that means more than enough. There is so much more grace than what is needed to meet every need; whatever you require, God has the grace for it, and more!

Conforming to the Creature

We want to be in the salt water of the Spirit, swimming in the purpose, plans and presence of God. Just like a sea turtle will struggle outside his natural environment, we can't thrive outside of God's will for our lives, living apart from the power and presence of His Spirit working in us. Paul tells us in Romans 12,

> "Therefore, I urge you, brothers, by the mercies of God, to present your bodies a living sacrifice, holy, acceptable to God, which is your spiritual service. Don't be conformed to this world, but be transformed by the renewing of your mind, so that you may prove what is the good, well-pleasing, and perfect will of God." (Romans 12:1-2, WEB)

This passage is the key to thriving in the will of God —don't be conformed to this world! To conform, in this passage, means to comply with the rules and standards of this world. However, we know that if the standard does not line up with the word of God, we are not to conform to it.

The apostle John writes to us warning us of the dangers of following the ways and mannerisms of this world:

> Don't love the world or the things that are in the world. If anyone loves the world, the Father's love isn't in him. For all that is in the world, the lust of the flesh, the lust of the eyes, and the pride of life, isn't the Father's, but is the world's. (1 John 2:15-16, WEB)

When we gravitate toward the things of this world, we have

less passion for the things of God; just the opposite happens as we move closer to God. Once you become a believer, swimming in the salt waters of his Spirit, you are no longer dominated by your flesh! "But you are not in the flesh but in the Spirit if it is so that the Spirit of God dwells in you" (Romans 8:9, WEB). You now have authority over your flesh! You are no longer a slave to the desires of fleshly appetites, but the tendency toward, and opportunity to, conform to the ways of the world is still there! We have to remain on guard. Even though we are in the Spirit, and He is in us, we still possess our own free will; the enemy will do everything he can to get you to conform to the pattern of this world, keeping you from being effective in the Kingdom of God.

I have been misled so many times by the things I see, and the things that have been impressed upon me, in the world. I'm seeing this happen more and more among believers. There are so many things in the world to tempt, distract, and influence us away from the will of God and His best plan for our lives. They seem to have an uncanny attraction about them, and these creatures seem to take on a life of their own. It's like the Devil puts a spell on the things of the world. Paul may have had the same idea when he asked the Galatian church, "Who has bewitched you?" (Galatians 3:1, WEB). The Greek word for bewitch is "baskainó," and it means to cast a spell, or to be spellbinding by appealing to someone's vanity and selfishness. That should cause us to sit up and pay close attention to what we allow to influence us. We can be bewitched in so many ways, by something we watch, something that is said to us, or something that appeals to our flesh. For me personally, this happens when I'm not keeping myself occupied with the affairs of the Kingdom of God. I may keep up with reading my Bible, or saying a few prayers, but the devotion becomes more mechanical and less rooted in a passion for God. That is when I am tempted by the world; it's just like letting your guard down in a fight.

I remember a time when physical fitness practically took over my life. It is not that physical fitness is a bad thing, or even a sin, it becomes a problem when it is all consuming — when it is top priority. This is true of anything! One year I got caught up in watching CrossFit games and the Titan games. I was so impressed with the physical appearance and athleticism of the competitors that I wanted to be built like them. I began a training routine, and even turned my garage into a gym. I had Olympic weights, medicine balls, bands, dip bars, and battle ropes. The sad thing is that my passion for physical fitness took over my passion for God. I was more concerned and consumed with my workout routines: what was going to be the workout of the day, what I was going to eat and how many calories of this and that. I was so consumed with my fitness program that I did not allow time for anything else. I was totally bewitched by wanting to conform to the world. We are finite beings, with only a certain amount to give. If we allow it to happen, anything can occupy our capacity for passion that we need to reserve for God!

During this season, I maintained going to church, tithing, and witnessing, however, my heart was getting farther and farther from God. After several months I realized I did not feel the strength of His peace and presence in my life. I felt far from God, and I knew that was not good. I started changing and rearranging my priorities by putting God first, and it wasn't long before my passion was reignited in my life through the knowledge and appreciation of His presence.

Worshipping the Creature

What I had done was create an idol in my life out of my workout routine and fitness goals. An idol is something you worship more than God. It gets the better part of your time, energy, money, attention, and all the other things that God should receive from us. When God is second, or third, or anything other than first, you're swimming in the fresh waters! Things will get more difficult the longer you're in those waters, and the real danger comes when we try and put God's name on our idol! Or when we attempt to worship Him and our idol at the same time.

Here is just one of a thousand examples: I've talked with so many men who knew they were outside of God's will, living in sin and fornicating with women. They would tell me how they thought that going to church would smooth things over! This thought process is far from the heart of God. Those activities and women are idols, and the men are living in disobedience. Listen to the words of God through Ezekiel,

> "Son of man, these men have taken their idols into their heart, and put the stumbling block of their iniquity before their face. Should I be inquired of at all by them?" (Ezekiel 14:3, WEB)

God is saying it would be futile to go before Him with something in our heart or in our lives that we are treating with more respect than Him, asking Him to bless it! That just sounds crazy typing it out, and probably seems crazy as you read it, but that's how far the insanity takes us when are deceived or bewitched by the things in the world.

Complementing the Creature

There is a natural progression that takes place as we conform to the world. We first begin to take on the image of the world, then we worship the image of the world, then we try to conform the image of what we are worshipping to the image of God. We have to understand this is a very grievous thing! As I was writing this, I was sharing some of the content with some co-workers, and two of them shared with me the same quote at different times, neither of them knowing that the other had said exactly the same thing. And it was this:

> The greatest complement God gave man was when He created him in His own image. The greatest insult was when man attempted to make God in his image.
> (Author Unknown)

Having two people separately share this same quote with me, the Holy Spirit was clearly showing me how we are conforming Jesus into our image. I did some research and here are some ways we have portrayed Jesus which do not match documented history or the reality of His character:

- a rich man who promotes the love of money
- a man who uses and misuses drugs and alcohol

- a man who is gay or transgender
- a man who is a violent, insolent rebel

So how did we get here? First of all, we have tried to change God into our image so that we won't have to change. Secondly, we are so afraid of offending people and losing church attendees that we compromise on what we say is truth. Third, we don't want to suffer persecution, so we paint Jesus in a different light to groups who might disagree with us. I'm sure the full list is extensive, but let's consider these the top three.

This is very dangerous ground because the Holy Spirit is working to conform us into the image of Jesus. If we do not worship the truth of who Jesus is, then we won't have the witness of the Holy Spirit; He is the Spirit of truth, and He will not support a lie. How this must grieve the Holy Spirit when we try and conform God the Son into our image, while God is wanting to conform us into Christ's image. We will only descend deeper into depravity if we continue to operate this way. There are churches out there that are promoting this kind of thinking claiming they are just trying to be diverse, or inclusive. But our Lord came to bring a sword!

> "Don't think that I came to send peace on the earth. I didn't come to send peace, but a sword." (Matthew 10:34, WEB)

Jesus wants us to pick a side. We can't conform to the world and worship him wholeheartedly, nor can we conform Him to the world to suit our needs. We are either for Him or we are against Him (Matthew 12:20). We are to serve Him, stand for Him and suffer with Him. Notice how it is a choice: "for

151

Him or against Him." There is no middle ground here. We are in a war against the kingdom of darkness; compromising would be treason. I'm not trying to shoot anyone down; in fact, I've learned a lot of these things from my own mistakes and experiences and want to help you break free from the lies of the enemy and experience the liberating power of God in Christ! I don't think any of us wake up planning to fail in our faith, or conform to the pattern of this world, or get caught up in sinful behaviors (i.e., backslide). This pattern of behavior generally starts out small before we find ourselves drifting at sea.

Driftwood

Most driftwood is either the whole or parts of trees that have been washed into the ocean due to flooding, high winds, erosion or other natural occurrences. The wood then drifts at sea, just going with the flow until it beaches somewhere in the world.

The same thing can happen to us when the storms of life come, or other natural occurrences cause us to take our eyes off of Jesus. We begin to drift at sea, going with the flow, going through the motions. Sometimes it starts out small, like the process of erosion: you miss a Sunday, your prayer life gets neglected, you start spending more time watching TV or on social media than in your Bible, and before you know it, you're under the influence of the world, the flesh, and the Devil. We end up bewitched by the things and passions of this world, and the love for the Father we had in Christ begins to lose its fire. The writer of Hebrews encourages us, saying:

Therefore let's also, seeing we are surrounded by so great a cloud of witnesses, lay aside every weight and the sin which so easily entangles us, and *let's run with perseverance the race that is set before us, looking to Jesus,* the author and perfecter of faith, who for the joy that was set before him endured the cross, despising its shame, and has sat down at the right hand of the throne of God. For consider him who has endured such contradiction of sinners against himself, that you don't grow weary, fainting in your souls (Hebrews 12:1-3, WEB).

When we find ourselves adrift, that is the time to rest in Jesus, to allow Him to hold us, to seek His peace, and His promises. If we keep our hearts and minds focused on Him, we won't be bewitched by the things of the world that distract and deceive us.

Transformation

When we are born again by the Spirit of God, we become new creatures in an instant, but our minds still need to be renewed, and that takes time. The old way of thinking and reasoning needs to change so that our thoughts and actions line up with the thoughts and actions that are revealed in the word of God. His thoughts reveal to us the fruit of His Spirit — what He desires for our lives. Paul says that we can actually be transformed, by renewing our minds (Romans 12:2). The Greek word for transform is "metamorpho," meaning to be changed from one thing into another. It's where we get the word metamorphosis, which is commonly used to describe a caterpillar when it changes into a butterfly.

Due to the rapid advancement in technology, there have been some major breakthroughs in understanding the human brain in recent decades. One thing that seems to be getting a lot of attention is how we can actually change our brains. Scientists have proven that your brain is being molded and changed by your experiences every day. This is referred to as neuroplasticity. I used to work in a factory where we made automotive parts out of plastic (e.g., gas tanks, air ducts, etc.), and we used a thermal forming machine. The plastic would go into an oven and once heated to the desired temperature, it would be brought back out and mechanically placed over a mold, which would transform the plastic into the shape of the mold as it cured.

Neuroplasticity works the same way, except with neurons, and neurotransmitters, and synapses instead of plastic, ovens, and molds; we can actually transform our minds by creating new habits and ways of thinking and responding.

I used to tell my wife I was "covering my tracks" whenever I would catch myself responding in a negative way. The reason I would say that is because, over time, our brain forms tracks or pathways from our thoughts and feelings. A neural pathway is a series of connected neurons that send signals from one part of the brain to another. Neurons come in three main types: motor neurons that control muscles; sensory neurons that are stimulated by our senses; and inter-neurons that connect neurons together. When we deliberately choose to think differently from the beaten path and begin to think and respond in line with the word of God, we are changing our brain and creating new pathways. Our brain likes to take the path of least resistance. The more times the same decision is made, the stronger that neural pathway becomes, until that decision is the quickest way to get from point A to point B in the brain. When we repeatedly choose the way of Christ, we change our brain to be more like Christ!

Navigating for a Change

I heard a preacher talk about how a study was done on the brains of London taxicab drivers. Researchers discovered that the hippocampus in the brain of these cab drivers had been enlarged. The hippocampus plays a critical role in the formation, organization, and storage of new memories, as well as connecting certain sensations and emotions to these memories. It is also thought to play an important role in spatial processing (i.e., relating to, or occupying, space) and navigation. Taxi drivers have so many streets, and attractions, and detours to remember that they have larger and plumper memory centers when compared to their peers. Studies also showed the longer they have been driving a taxi the larger the hippocampus! They physically and mentally transformed their brains by learning to navigate through the streets of London! As we navigate through this world, how much more will our minds be transformed as we memorize and meditate on the word of God?!?

This is how we learn to navigate our way through every

circumstance and situation in such a way that our lives line up with the will of God for lives. Paul tells us in Romans,

> "Don't be *conformed* to this world, but be *transformed* by the renewing of your mind, so that you may prove *what is the good, well pleasing, and perfect will* of God." (Romans 12:2, WEB)

The Will of the Sea

We renew our minds by meditating upon, studying, and applying the word of God to our lives. As we renew our minds, we learn to discern the will of God for our lives. The will of God has dimensions that are beyond our understanding and at times the Holy Spirit will reveal hidden things to us about His will. However, when I think of the will of God, I focus on four aspects of his will: His *preceptive* will, His *permissive* will, His *personal* will, and His *perfect* will.

His *preceptive* will is what He has clearly revealed in His word for our lives. For example, "love one another," would be His preceptive will for your life because it's one of His precepts that He has clearly revealed in His word. His *permissive* will is the freewill He has given to humanity. We are free to choose the paths we take in life, but we are not free from the consequences of our choices. His *personal* will is His will for your life as an individual. God's calling for each of us is unique. The Apostle Paul was set apart as a herald for the Gospel. Mother Teresa had a calling to look after the poor. God's personal will is His will for your life. However, it does not exclude or separate you from other believers; you are a part of a body of believers. *God equips us in such a way that each part of the body benefits another part.* (Romans 12:3-8). Finally, His *perfect* will. His perfect will is found in you, when you are operating under the whole counsel, plans, and purposes that He has for your life.

Following the Truth to your Destiny

As you choose to follow the preceptive will of God for all believers, you will eventually discover His personal will for your life. It's a natural progression that occurs as we follow the **red light** for our lives. I've seen this happen in my life and the life of others. If at some point along the way it seems you don't know what to do, just do the next right thing.

I like to journal events and seasons in my life, especially times when God is on the move. For a season in my life, I kept track of about five years with a lot of detail involving events and occurrences where I felt God was leading me in a specific direction. When I put it all together at the end of that season, I could see the hand of God guiding me in striking detail, so much so that I was able draw a chart and use it in a sermon to illustrate how He leads us into the plans and purposes He has for our lives. What I discovered is this: *He leads us in one obedient act after another.* Every time you obey God in a certain area, you move closer to all that He has for your life. That is the perfect will of God for your life!

CHARTER GUIDE NINE
"Salt Waters or Fresh Waters"

Your ninth choice is to either *Swim in the Salt Waters of your Destiny* or *follow the Fresh waters of the World*.

- Reflect on some times in your life when you were swimming upstream (i.e., against God's ways and His plans for your life).

- What people or things of this world have bewitched you during different seasons of your life?

- What are some ways you may have tried to change the image of God to match some "thing" or some "one" or a "lifestyle," in order to match your own desires and thinking?

- What does it look like when you are just "drifting along" in your spiritual life?

- Have you experienced any changes or transformations in your life as a result of studying and applying God's word to your life?

- Which of the four types of God's will (preceptive, permissive, personal, and perfect) do you feel you are experiencing in your life and why?

THE CHOICE

You have to choose to either *Swim in the Salt Waters of your Destiny* or follow the *Fresh waters of the World.*

Scripture: "Don't be *conformed* to this world, but be *transformed* by the renewing of your mind, so that you may prove *what is the good, well pleasing, and perfect will* of God." -Romans 12:2, WEB

Thought: Jesus wants us to pick a side. We can't conform to the world and worship him wholeheartedly, nor can we conform Him to the world to suit our needs. We are either for Him or we are against Him.

NOTE:

Choice Ten

Breathe

Even though sea turtles were created for the ocean, they are still reptiles; therefore they need to come up for air periodically. However, they can stay underwater for several hours without taking a breath. It all depends on their level of activity. Similarly, our spirits need to breathe. A preacher who mentored me for season would say to me, "Prayer is to the spirit what breath is to the body." Prayer is vital in the life of the believer, so much so that, if neglected, your spiritual life with God suffers.

We can pray for anything:

- Pray for knowledge of His will. 1 John 5:14
- Pray for the lost. 1 John 5:15
- Pray for strength. 1 Chronicles 16:4

- Pray for restoration in your home, city, church, and country. 2 Chronicles 7:14
- Pray for enlightenment. Ephesians 1:18
- Pray on all occasions with all kinds of requests. Ephesians 6:18
- Pray when you're in trouble or need healing. James 5:13
- Pray for your enemies. Matthew 5:44
- Pray for ANYTHING. Mark 11:24

I have heard it said, (and this is not a direct quote), that little prayer time equals little kingdom power. However, much prayer time equals much kingdom power! I find that so challenging because I'm such a "do-er." I can't sit still for very long before I have to get moving. Even when I'm reading, I have to have something going on in the background because I just don't do well at being still.

Prayer has been a very challenging discipline for me, and I have learned some lessons along the way. I have to admit, I envy those who can pray long and bold prayers. I have tried to mimic preachers who pray loud, bold, passionate prayers. As I look back, my attempts to imitate those prayers were just superficial. They were not birthed out of my own passion and experiences. The Holy Spirit is not going to respond based on how well we perform in prayer, He is going to respond to how real we are when we pray. We had a family member on my wife's side of the family who was terminally ill. I did not know her that well, but I felt led to go pray for her. I pictured myself going over there full of faith and power in the Holy Spirit! After all, it was God asking me to go pray for her. I'm sorry to say, the blunders of my flesh know no bounds! My wife and I drove over to meet with the family. Once we arrived and I saw the condition of her aunt, and her aunt's family preparing for the worst, it suffocated the fire in me!

I went limp at this point. I didn't even *want* to pray, let alone know *how* or *what* to pray. The time came for us leave, and my wife asked me "Are you going to pray?" I said I would, so we went into the room where she was laying, and we all gathered around her, and I prayed. It was not a bold, loud, powerful, commanding prayer; it was more like "Oh God help, because I'm way out of my league!" I prayed for healing and comfort and whatever else I could think of in the moment, and then we left.

I felt somewhat defeated. However, two days later, we received a phone call that she was doing better. That lasted for a season, then she was once again bed ridden and the family was called to say their goodbyes. My wife and I went to see her, and it was amazing! She was prophesying and seeing friends and family members in heaven! She prophesied to my wife about our grandchildren, and she was spot on! She even gave me a word of confirmation about something I had been praying about —that only God knew — she confirmed it without even knowing! She was seeing heaven. She kept talking about a door, and how everyone needs to read their Bible every day.

It was interesting to me that she mentioned a door. The gospels record Jesus speaking of a door:

> When once the master of the house has risen up, and has shut *the door*, and you begin to stand outside and to knock at the door, saying, "Lord, Lord, open to us!" (Luke 13:25, WEB)

And in Matthew we read:

> While they went away to buy, the bridegroom came, and those who were ready went in with him to the wedding feast, and *the door* was shut. Afterward the other virgins also came, saying, "Lord, Lord, open to us." (Matthew 25:10-11, WEB)

What this woman was seeing was a revelation for sure! The door could represent the time of grace we are in, and the time we have to enter, or it could be a literal door. The point is how much she stressed the door and to stay in the word of God! Looking back on that experience, I can say God answered my prayer with signs and wonders. The Lord also revealed to us that she is now with Him. Even though I did not pray a bold, commanding prayer, I did pray a real, genuine prayer. Jesus warned us not to pray for show, "And when you pray, do not be like the hypocrites, for they love to pray standing in the synagogues and on the street corners to be seen by others. Truly I tell you, they have received their reward in full (Matthew 6:5, WEB)." Have I ever prayed for show? Yes. And it went down just like the Master said it would. However, there have been times when I prayed boldly in public, and God moved.

I remember a time when I was preaching, and I didn't realize until a few minutes into the sermon that I had not prayed for God's anointing on the message. I stopped mid-message and told the congregation I needed to pray for the Holy Spirit's help. I prayed, and when I did it was like I could see a mist just fall on everyone! When the message was over, a man told me

I could have preached for another hour! It was an awesome move of God. But there have been other times when I prayed before preaching just so I could appear spiritual! Not only was that pathetic, but I also felt totally powerless while preaching. I want to be painfully honest with you because I want everyone who reads this to find freedom, and to see how patient God is with us! I can see now that I was praying more for a show than from the heart, and the times when I have done this I have had a very difficult time delivering the message. When it was all over, I realized what I had done and made the decision that I will either pray a real heartfelt prayer without concern for how others think of it, or I will have someone pray before the service. Prayer is not a show, it is communicating with God, who requires our honesty and is worthy of reverence and worship.

Prayer can be powerful and specific. There have been times when I have prayed for revelation about scripture and God would just download so much wisdom in me that I would have to pray that it stopped! There will be times when the Spirit prays through us. When that happens, you may feel a deep burden or groaning in your Spirit. I had this experience for years; at times I would be practically doubled over because I was feeling such a burden in my gut, but afterward I would feel incredible peace in my spirit.

Tears in the Sea

Sea turtles secrete excess salt from the salt glands behind their eyes. This allows them to live in the salty ocean and maintain lower concentrations of salt inside their bodies. Because the excessive salt is flushed out through their eyes it gives the appearance that they are crying. This is healthy! And so is our own emotional release. Sometimes we may be moved to tears when the Holy Spirit is praying through us or is burdened. The Bible says Jesus would pray with loud cries. "He, in the days of his flesh, having offered up prayers and petitions with strong crying and tears to him who was able to save him from death" (Hebrews 5:7, WEB).

Now that He is risen, it is His Spirit living in us that enables us to share His burdens. Years ago, I was living out of town away from my family and friends. I remember a time when I was talking with a friend on the phone, and when the conversation was over I was so moved that I burst into tears. I knew at the time was he lost and addicted to drugs, alcohol, and other vices. Because I was so moved emotionally, I knew it had to be the Spirit of God in me. I'm not easily moved, and I had known about my friend's addiction for years and was never grieved over it. I was weeping over his soul, and the fact that he was lost. I could feel how God's heart was broken for him. Jesus said in John 3:16 that "God so loved the world that he *gave*." I've heard it said, *"You can give and not love, but you can't love and not give."* God so loved that he *gave*. God loves you and He wants a relationship with you. He desires to talk with you, even through your tears, and wants to give your life meaning and purpose.

Tongues

Sea turtles have tongues, but they can't stick their tongues out to catch food. Similarly, not all believers speak in tongues. I know some will argue, but hear me out. Speaking in tongues is basically a prayer-like practice where the person is speaking out loud, but in a language that no one readily understands. This can be a very sensitive topic because some believe if you can't speak in tongues, you are not saved. I have read the Bible, and that statement is not found in scriptures anywhere. By definition, tongues are a *gift of the Spirit,* not the saving grace that is imputed *by* the Spirit. In fact, the Bible says tongues will cease. "Love never fails. But where there are prophecies, they will be done away with. *Where there are various languages, they will cease.* Where there is knowledge, it will be done away with" (1 Corinthians 13:8, TPT). Love is enduring, but tongues will one day *cease.* The evidence of salvation is seen in the *fruit* of the Spirit, which is love, Paul says,

> "But the *fruit* of the Spirit is love, joy, peace, patience, kindness, goodness, faith, gentleness, and self-control. Against such things there is no law" (Galatians 5:22-23, WEB).

Those two passages reveal to us that the evidence of salvation is seen in the *fruit* of the Spirit not in the *gifts of the* Spirit. I have prayed for the gift of tongues. I've even traveled to apostolic churches in search of the gift! I have prayed for the gift every time a TV preacher would claim to be imparting the gift, which by the way isn't theologically sound. The only one who can distribute gifts is the Holy Spirit, and they are distributed as *He determines.* "But the one and the same Spirit produces all of these, *distributing to each one separately as he desires*" (1 Corinthians 12:11, WEB). So, save your money the next time someone asks you to sow a seed so you can receive a spiritual gift — that decision belongs to the Holy Spirit.

I prayed about this gift and was asking God why people speak in tongues and for what purpose. I had heard that the purpose of speaking in a tongue was so that the Devil would not know what God was saying, but the Bible says someone needs to be able to interpret the tongue. Now, if someone interprets the tongue it is no longer a secret to anybody, everyone will know. I'm not trying to shoot anyone down; I'm just explaining the logic and principles behind speaking in tongues, according to scripture. I've also been in a service where people were speaking in tongues, but there was no one to interpret what was being said. My reaction was "How is this benefiting anyone?" Through all my prayer and seeking, the Lord said to me, "The purpose for praying in a tongue is so the *person speaking* won't know what he or she is saying, so that their mind cannot argue with what the Spirit is saying."

Here is an example: one of my friends was in a church service when someone stood up and started speaking to him in a tongue, and then someone else stood up and interpreted it. The interpreter told him that the Spirit said, "He is being stubborn!" If I was the one speaking in tongues, and I knew what I was about to say, there would be a wrestling match going on in my mind about whether or not that was really what the Spirit was saying; however, if I had no idea what I was saying, I could speak objectively. This is one of the gifts of tongues given through the Holy Spirit. Another type of speaking in tongues is in a foreign language. I knew a man who was in a prayer circle when someone in the circle started speaking to him in a foreign language and no one knew what the man was saying except my friend. He said the man was speaking in his native language. You don't need an interpreter when that happens.

Fasting and Prayer

During the summer months, sea turtles eat an estimated 73 percent of their own body weight daily; that would be around 16,000 calories a day! I don't know about you, but if I eat one ounce of chocolate, I gain a pound! Now, a sea turtle is going to spend a lot of time searching for food to consume that many calories. We simply aren't used to the idea of searching further than our own refrigerator for food, but in Biblical times, if you wanted to eat, you had to hunt for it. To keep your food fresh, you had to keep it alive. You didn't kill your food until you were ready to cook it, so a lot of time would be spent preparing meals. Today you can throw your dinner in the microwave and have it in a matter of minutes, so fasting food really just seems like going hungry for Jesus. But fasting food in Biblical times definitely allowed for more time to seek the Lord. For me personally, the times I've fasted food, or did something like a Daniel fast, all I could think about was food! I've even gone several days with no food, with God's help. But fasting food has never produced the same revival in my spirit as I have experienced when I've fasted from TV or some other time-consuming activity to seek Him. There is no right or wrong thing to fast from, it is the heart of the practice of fasting that matters. However, I do believe food is a big one.

It's worth noting that God rewards those who seek Him,

> "Without faith it is impossible to be well pleasing to him, for he who comes to God must believe that he exists, *and that he is a rewarder of those who seek him*" (Hebrews 11:6, WEB).

Some people may fast when something tragic happens, or when the Holy Spirit moves on them to fast. Once, I was at work when a man I didn't know very well came up to me and said he had a word for me; he told me what God had put on his heart to share with me, and it definitely spoke to me. After our conversation, I did not see him for a few days. A short time later, I met up with him again and we were talking about the word he gave me. He went on to share with me how nervous he was about telling me, even though what he had to share was a Good Word! He said as soon as he finished speaking with me, he fasted for three days. He hadn't planned in advance to fast, it just spontaneously happened. Here's the beauty: God rewarded His obedience and discipline. See, he told me he was a diabetic — and he no longer needed his insulin shots after the fast!

Pray

Prayer is not always something you sit down and do in a quiet space. It's something that continues throughout your day. The Bible says we are to "pray without ceasing" (1 Thessalonians

5:17). We should be in constant communication with God. A person who prays without ceasing has made a habit of communicating one-on-one with God. Prayer is to our spirit what breath is to our life.

You may need to set aside a prayer time each day. Depending on what is going on in your life, there will be times when you pray more than others. Daniel was one of the major prophets in the Old Testament, and he regularly prayed three times a day and was given great revelations and knowledge of many things. Jesus also had a disciplined prayer life, even though He was and is God. Remember, He was fully human during His time on Earth, and He knew the critical importance of prayer and the impact it would have on His life. Prayer is an essential part of our lives.

Sometimes we think, why pray if God already knows what I need? I think of it like how I communicate with my children and grandchildren. I know what their needs are, but I still want to interact with them and hear what they have to say, even when I know what they want. In the same way, we are God's children; even though God already knows what you are going to say, and what you will and ask for, He still wants to hear from you and interact with you, and answer your prayers, and give you revelation and wisdom.

The Model Prayer

One of the disciples of Jesus asked Him how to pray. And Jesus said to them:

When you pray, say:

"Father, hallowed be your name, your kingdom come.

Give us each day our daily bread.

Forgive us our sins, for we also forgive everyone who sins against us.

And lead us not into temptation." (Luke 11:2-4, NIV)

This is how Jesus taught us to pray, so let's break it down,

The Father

Personally, it is difficult to see God as my Father, because I did not have a Father growing up. My father passed away when I was very young, so I don't have anything to which I can compare a father-son relationship. I find it difficult just to see how the role of a father functions in a relationship. Now, I am a father and grandfather, and I know I have fallen far short as a father, but I have certainly learned a lot along the way. Maybe you are in a similar situation; maybe you did not have a father-figure, or parents growing up. Maybe you experienced abuse from a parent or father figure. Maybe you don't feel worthy of the love of a father.

Those experiences are real. But, be encouraged, God is the *perfect* Father! His love is perfect, and He loves you perfectly and eternally! "The LORD appeared to us in the past, saying: *"I have loved you with an everlasting love; I have drawn you with unfailing kindness"* (Jeremiah 31:3, NIV). God loves you eternally! He thinks more about you than you do, and the plans

He has for your life go right on into eternity! Because He is God, He is the perfect Father, and He wants us to be in a Parent-child relationship with Him. Isn't that amazing?!? When we approach Him in prayer, we can be confident in His love, concern, and care for us. You don't have to worry about anyone's opinion of you. You don't need to appear important, or achieve some level of success, or be gifted or talented. You are perfectly loved by a perfect Father who is able to make all grace abound to you!

The Greatness of God

Think about who God is. He is infinite and all powerful in everything. He knows everything. He is eternal. He is the creator of everything. Just think about the size of our universe; it cannot be measured, or even comprehended, yet God says he stretched out the heavens by the width of His hand.

> "Who has measured the waters *of the sea* in the hollow of his hand and used his hand-width to mark off the heavens? Who knows the exact weight of all the dust of the earth and has weighed all the mountains and hills on his scale?" (Isaiah 40:12, TPT)

That just blows my mind! The universe is the width of His hand. That doesn't mean God actually held out a hand that could be measured, because God is Spirit, and He is infinite in every aspect of His being. What it means, though, is that He knows the boundaries of the universe. There is nothing that exists outside of God.

Whether seen or unseen, whatever is brought into existence exists in God, because there is nothing outside of God. He is the only infinite being in existence. There cannot be two infinite beings. If there was more than one, they would no longer be infinite! To say there are two infinite beings in any aspect is an oxymoron. To be God means you have no equal or rival. "To whom then will you liken me? Who is my equal?" says the Holy One (Isaiah 40:25, WEB). Everything exists in God and there is nothing outside of Him or beyond Him. He has no beginning and no end; He is beyond everything and fills everything! I get overwhelmed when I think about the greatness of God. I'm filled with this feeling of awe when I think about how great God is, just within the limitations of my own mind. God is not someone we can fully comprehend though, because our minds are finite where He is infinite.

This is the mindset we should have when we approach God in prayer. He is our Father, but He is also God. When Jesus says, "hallowed be your name," it means we come to Him with reverence. We need to recognize that God is set apart from everything and everyone. He is holy, awesome, and worthy of honor and praise because He is God almighty. That sounds intimidating, but it should give us boldness! That is our Father! Paul says, "What then shall we say about these things? If God is for us, who can be against us?" (Romans 8:31, WEB). You are His child! It is hard to even wrap our minds around all that means!

Our Needs

Jesus prompts us to ask for "our daily bread" (i.e., our needs). God promises to meet our needs, but never guarantees we are going to get everything we want. He knows that not everything we want is going to be good for us. James puts it this way:

> You don't have because you don't ask. You ask, and don't receive, because you ask with wrong motives, so that you may spend it on your pleasures. You adulterers and adulteresses, don't you know that friendship with the world is hostility toward God? (James 4:2-4, WEB)

We are not going to get everything we ask for. James says if our affections are for the things of this world, we should not expect to receive something that will put a wedge between us and our Father. He won't give us something that will cause us to feel hostile toward Him!

There have been times when I have had to say no to my kids when they wanted something because I knew would not be good for them, and, of course, they would get upset with me over it. I was not upset with them, but they were upset with me because I said "no." They did not realize that what I was doing was out of love for them, and I was doing what was best for them. When we want something that will take us away from the heart of God, we're asking for something that will be harmful to us; so, God says "no," just like a good parent. Then we get mad because our affections for the world are greater than our affection for our Father. We need to evaluate what our hearts are set on, making the adjustments needed to get back into fellowship with the one who loves us. I really think that is why we sometimes struggle with God — He loves us more than we love ourselves!

Forgive

Next, Jesus says we are to "forgive everyone who sins against us". Paul says, "Be kind to one another, tender hearted, *forgiving each other, just as God also in Christ forgave you*" (Ephesians 4:32, WEB). Just think about what you have been forgiven of. If you have trouble forgiving, it could be because you don't recognize and appreciate the depth of God's forgiveness to you. Jesus asked a Pharisee named Simon this question:

> "A certain lender had two debtors. The one owed five hundred denarii, and the other fifty. When they couldn't pay, he forgave them both. Which of them therefore will love him most?" Simon answered, "I suppose to whom he forgave the most." (Luke 7:41-43, WEB)

Jesus went on to explain that someone who has been forgiven much loves much, and whoever has been forgiven little loves little. Here's the thing: we have all been forgiven much! The truth is, though, not everyone realizes how much they have been forgiven. We have to be "cut deep" like we talked about before, when it comes to understanding the weight of our own forgiveness. When someone offends us, or asks us for forgiveness, we need to forgive them. If we hold on to offenses, it gives the Devil a foothold in our lives. This takes us right into the last thing Jesus mentions in His model prayer.

Tempted and Tried

Jesus said we are to pray that we will not be led into temptation. This word "temptation" in the Greek could mean two things. It could mean you're being tempted to sin, or you're being tested by going through a trial (i.e., to test your character). The Devil is the author of temptation, not God. James tells us,

> "Let no man say when he is tempted, 'I am tempted by God,' *for God can't be tempted* by evil, *and he himself tempts no one.* But each one is tempted when he is drawn away by his own lust and enticed." (James 1:13-14, WEB)

Satan does the tempting. James points out how he tempts us with our own lusts and desires (vs. 14). The Devil only appeals to us through the things we already like; he tempts us with the hopes that we will take the bait and fail to do what God has called us to do. He attempted this in the wilderness with Jesus; he tempted Him with several things trying to get Him to sin, and to fail in His mission. So, the Devil tempts us to trip us up.

There is a difference between being tempted and being tested, however. The second meaning of the Greek word for tempted, where we are tested through trials is under God's authorship. When God tests us, His goal is to promote us. He is testing us to determine if our spiritual maturity will allow us to handle more responsibility. God considers testing necessary, not to lead us into an evil act, but to afford us the chance to gain experience and strength. The Bible says that Jesus was led by the Spirit into the wilderness to be tempted (Luke 4). The word "tempted" in this verse comes from the same root word for temptation used in the Lord's Prayer. God was allowing the temptation from Satan for the purpose of testing, to prove that Jesus was, and is, the Son of God. After the tempter left him, Luke says Jesus came out of the wilderness in the *power* of the Spirit (Luke 4:14). This happened just before Jesus began His public ministry. Before He could begin His *public* ministry, He had to conquer a *private* battle. We face the same challenge: we cannot move on to greater authority, power, and position until we have passed the tests.

Staying connected to God in prayer is the best way to get through anything life throws at us, and it's a way to grow your relationship with God. Like the sea turtles understand their need for breath, we have to understand our need for prayer. We were created to live in relationship with our Father, to communicate with Him regularly, one-on-one.

CHARTER GUIDE TEN
"Breathe"

Your tenth choice is to either *breathe the air of heaven* or *suffocate in silence*.

- On a scale of one to ten, how would you rate your prayer life?

- Do you feel you pray with confidence? *Jesus said, "Therefore I tell you, all things whatever you pray and ask for, believe that you have received them, and you shall have them." (Mark 11:24, WEB)*

- Have there been times when you recognized God had answered your prayers?

- What do you think about praying in a foreign language or a heavenly language?

- Do you struggle to see God as Your Father and why?

- What keeps you from making prayer a priority in your life?

- What is God saying to you about entrusting you with greater responsibility?

THE CHOICE

You have to choose to either *breathe the air of heaven* or *suffocate in silence.*

Scripture: The Bible says we are to "pray without ceasing" (1 Thessalonians 5:17).

Thought: "Prayer is to the spirit what breath is to the body." Prayer is vital in the life of the believer, so much so that, if neglected, your spiritual life with God suffers.

NOTES:

Choice Eleven

The Empty Shell

J ust like sea turtles, we will all one day depart from our shell. The Apostle Peter refers to his physical body as a tent. "I think it right, as long as I am in this *tent,* to stir you up by reminding you, knowing that the *putting off of my tent* comes swiftly, even as our Lord Jesus Christ made clear to me" (2 Peter 1:14, WEB). He knew his life was passing; however, he also knew it would not be the end of his life, but only the beginning.

> The apostle John writes, "These things I have written to you who believe in the name of the Son of God, that you may know that you have *eternal life*, and that you may continue to believe in the name of the Son of God." (1 John 5:13, WEB)

We will live forever; the end of our physical life is only the beginning of our eternal life. *Where* we live forever is a choice. Eternity only gives us two options, Heaven or Hell, and we have to choose for ourselves which one. I will never forget the time I was in the home of a woman who was about to die. The family had been called to come and say their goodbyes. This woman was actually lingering between heaven and earth. At the time they called some of the relatives in she was seeing loved ones in heaven and wanted to share the experience with everyone. At one point, she began to see another family member, who was not in heaven. It was the father of these children who were now adults. The father was asking for forgiveness, and the woman who was passing away was telling the children that they had to forgive him, (he abused the children severely when they were young). She was struggling to understand why she could not get to the man to bring him where she was going. I knew why, however, that's when things got difficult for me. One of the family members asked me why the father could not be with the family in heaven. Another member of the family said that they did not understand why he wasn't in heaven because he went to church. All I could say is, "We have to live out our faith." *(I was totally caught off guard!)*

The Bible does not acknowledge a faith that does not lead to obedience. James tells us in his letter, "faith apart from works is dead" (James 2:26, WEB). In light of that experience, I am now convinced more than ever that there is no purgatory where you stay until you're ready for heaven; you can't be prayed out or bought out. In fact, there is no mention of it in scripture anywhere. The Bible says, "Inasmuch as it is appointed for men to *die once*, and after this, *judgment*" (Hebrews 9:27, WEB). There is no reincarnation, no virgins waiting. When your body dies, your spirit endures; only our spirits will reside until the resurrection of our bodies. If you think about the anatomy of our being, we cannot come back as something other than what we are. It would be like saying a whale is ant — the two are incompatible. Your spirit is made for your body which is the exact representation of your being; it cannot accommodate something other than what it was created for, or it would no longer be you. You cannot come back as an ant, because your spirit is the eternal part of *your* being, and it is not compatible with something of a different design; reincarnation is not even logical when it comes to spiritual things comprised of eternal matter. It's just the Devil scrambling the truth about eternity to take people to Hell with him.

In the book of Revelation, John writes how the Devil deceived the nations! "Satan will be released from his prison, and he will come out to *deceive the nations* which are in the four corners of the earth" (Revelation 20:7-8, WEB). Not only does he deceive the nations (people in general), but Jesus also warned that he might even deceive the elect (those who follow Christ)! "For there will arise false Christs, and false prophets, and they will show great signs and wonders, so as to lead astray, if possible, even the chosen ones" (Matthew 24:24, NLT). Jesus also said that there will be those who knew the Lord (or at least knew about Him), and they will be shocked in one of two ways on the Day of Judgment.

Shell Shocked

Years ago, I set out to do some prison ministry, preaching and teaching inside facilities where men were incarcerated. I remember being in prayer about a particular service that was coming up, and the message I was going to bring. As I was in prayer about the service, I kept hearing the Lord say to me, "I will see you there." I didn't know what to expect, or what He meant by it. I began thinking there might be a big move of the Spirit during the service, or a powerful anointing. The day came to go to the facility, and I preached the message, and it was an awesome service! The message was definitely inspired and anointed. However, I did not *see the Lord"* like I had expected during the service.

It was not until after the service was over while I was talking with one of the inmates that I understood what He meant. While we were talking, what the Lord had been saying to me came to my mind, and that's when it hit me! I understood what He meant, because this scripture came to my mind as I remembered His words:

> Then the King will say to those on his right, "Come, you who are blessed by my Father; take your inheritance, the kingdom prepared for you since the creation of the world. For I was hungry, and you gave me something to eat, I was thirsty and you gave me something to drink, I was a stranger and you invited me in, I needed clothes and you clothed me, I was sick and you looked after me, **I was in prison and you came to visit me.**" Then the righteous will answer him, "Lord, when did we see you hungry and feed you, or thirsty and give you something to drink? When did we **see you** a stranger and invite you

in, or needing clothes and clothe you? When did we *see you* sick or in prison and go to visit you?"

The King will reply, "Truly I tell you, *whatever you did for one of the least of these brothers and sisters of mine, you did for me.*" (Matthew 25:31-40, NIV)

I was shocked! In a good way! What He meant by, "*I will see you there,*" was that I would see Him in the inmates. However, it wasn't until after the service that I realized it! I wonder how many opportunities we miss to serve Him through serving others because we think it is beneath us, or it's too menial, or it's not done in the spotlight. The flipside of that is to consider how many times have we have served someone and did not realize it was Him! Now for the other shock. Jesus said there would be another group that would go into shock at the judgment.

Then he will say to those on his left, "Depart from me, you who are cursed, into the eternal fire prepared for the devil and his angels. For I was hungry and you gave me nothing to eat, I was thirsty and you gave me nothing to drink, I was a stranger and you did not invite me in, I needed clothes and you did not clothe me, I was sick and in prison and you did not look after me."

They also will answer, "Lord, when did we see you hungry or thirsty or a stranger or needing clothes or sick or in prison, and did not help you?"

He will reply, "Truly I tell you, whatever you did not do for one of the least of these, you did not do for me."

Then they will go away to eternal punishment, but the righteous to eternal life. (Matthew 25:41-46, NIV)

Sometimes, *Jesus is the stranger in our own homes.* It's like the story of the father who knew about the Lord but did not look after the people closest to him. On another note, it's easy to help people who can help us, or at least one day return the favor, but what about those who cannot pay it back, or seem to be an inconvenience? What about doing good to those who do not deserve it? Jesus said we are to love our enemies and pray for those who persecute us (Matt.:44); that is how we win people for the kingdom.

Turtle Wax

I could not resist working in this heading! We want to shine our shells this side of heaven by preparing for eternity, because *our lives here are only a vapor in time.* James says,

"For what is your life? For you are a vapor that appears for a little time, and then vanishes away" (James 4:14, WEB).

The older I get, the quicker it seems time goes by. And the older I get, the more deliberate I am to live with fewer regrets

— not that anyone wants to live with regrets — but I think as we age, we put more thought into the decisions we make, especially when we put them in the light of eternity. We want to focus on the things that will last forever. Our, relationships will last forever. How we treat people in our lives will have eternal consequences. What we did to advance the kingdom will carry with it rewards. We should focus on what is going to last forever, so that we will not be ashamed once we step into eternity.

Jesus tells us to live in light of eternity:

> Don't lay-up treasures for yourselves on the earth, where moth and rust consume, and where thieves break through and steal; but lay up for yourselves treasures in heaven, where neither moth nor rust consume, and where thieves don't break through and steal; for where your treasure is, there your heart will be also. (Matthew 6:19-21, WEB)

My Pastor has a saying, "treat your body like you are going to live forever; treat your spirit like you are going to die tomorrow." Isn't that a good perspective? We don't know when God is going to call us to account, so if we live every day like it is our last, we live wiser. One of the most sobering things about the Day of Judgment is that we do not get another chance to live our lives this side of heaven again. We only have a short time to make the most of our time, and the judgment will last forever.

Buried Treasure

Jesus gave us another parable on how to prepare for eternity. He says:

> For it is like a man going into another country, who called his own servants and entrusted his goods to them. To one he gave five talents, to another two, to another one, to each according to his own ability. Then he went on his journey. Immediately he who received the five talents went and traded with them and made another five talents. In the same way, he also who got the two gained another two. But he who received the one talent went away and dug in the earth and hid his lord's money. (Matthew 25:14-18, WEB)

He says it's like a man going away on a journey. Jesus is using as an analogy for the time following His resurrection, when He returns to the Father for a season. He says he gave to each one according to their ability. The Lord told me once in prayer "I cannot give you more than you can give back to Me." God cannot give us any more than what we surrender, because whatever we cannot let go of is holding on to us. Beyond that, we are accountable for what we have been given.

So, the man gave his servants talents. A talent was a unit of measurement for weighing precious metals, usually gold and silver. So, he is entrusting each man with a certain amount of wealth. But in this parable, Jesus could be using talents to signify a spiritual gift or an actual talent, in addition to material wealth. The man who only received one talent buried it instead of investing it in the kingdom. He may have thought, because it was such a small amount compared to the others that it would not amount to much. If we can't see the value in what God has given us, we won't appreciate His abundance. The man wasted his talent by burying it instead of trying to multiply it.

Another one of my blunders was when I wanted to play the piano. My mother played for years, and I had some lessons, but I never got serious about it until I ran into some co-workers who were in a worship band. I thought I would join and just play some chords on the electric piano. After going to some practices, I learned I had a long way to go! I began spending a lot of time practicing and taking lessons. Once again, I found myself sacrificing time that could have been used to cultivate what I'm really gifted at. My spiritual gift is to preach and teach, but I was spending my time studying music theory instead of theology. As I continued down this path, it was getting harder instead of easier. There would be times we would be playing in a worship service, and everything would be working properly except for my equipment!

It all came to an end one night after a men's meeting at church. Our pastor was meeting with several men that he had asked to preach while he was away on a mission trip. In the meeting he gave everyone 3 passages of scripture to choose from and then we were to turn the scripture into a sermon. As soon as I saw the list, I knew which verse I was going to choose, and I had the sermon ready in a matter of minutes. To make a long story short, after the meeting was over, I was driving my car to meet some of the guys for dinner. On the way there the Lord reminded me of a documentary that I had seen on *60 Minutes* just a few weeks prior. There was an anchorman interviewing a young girl who was a prodigy on the piano. The interviewer had a hat with several notes in it; she told him to pick four notes and she would compose a piece of music for him. The anchorman pulls four notes out of the hat at random, and she composes a piece of music in minutes! As I was remembering that moment the Lord said to me, "Just like that girl picked four notes to compose a song, you did the same thing with one scripture to write a sermon," and then He added, "You're wasting your gift." I had been spending my time on a talent I did not have, at the expense of the talent I did have, and so I was burying my talent. After He corrected me, I repented and then He blessed me with more opportunities to use my gift.

Now, let's look at how the other servants handled the wealth entrusted to them:

> Now after a long time the lord of those servants came and settled accounts with them. He who received the five talents came and brought another five talents, saying, "Lord, you delivered to me five talents. Behold, I have gained another five talents in addition to them."

> His lord said to him, "Well done, good and faithful servant. You have been faithful over a few things, I will set you over many things. Enter into the joy of your lord."

> He also who got the two talents came and said, "Lord, you delivered to me two talents. Behold, I have gained another two talents in addition to them."

His lord said to him, "Well done, good and faithful servant. You have been faithful over a few things. I will set you over many things. Enter into the joy of your lord."

He also who had received the one talent came and said, "Lord, I knew you that you are a hard man, reaping where you didn't sow, and gathering where you didn't scatter. I was afraid and went away and hid your talent in the earth. Behold, you have what is yours."

But his lord answered him, "You wicked and slothful servant. You knew that I reap where I didn't sow and gather where I didn't scatter. You ought therefore to have deposited my money with the bankers, and at my coming I should have received back my own with interest. Take away therefore the talent from him and give it to him who has the ten talents. For to everyone who has will be given, and he will have abundance, but from him who doesn't have, even that which he has will be taken away. Throw out the unprofitable servant into the outer darkness, where there will be weeping and gnashing of teeth." (Matthew 25:19-30, WEB)

We will either be rewarded like the faithful servants or lose rewards like the lazy servant. I wonder how many opportunities the lazy servant missed to invest that one talent into someone's life. Who knows, he could have multiplied it one hundred-fold!

I've made it a point to weigh things in light of eternity. How much of my time, energy, and resources do I want to invest in business, relationships, ministries, and extracurricular activities? In making my decisions, I ask myself how these things will benefit the kingdom of God, and my life and others in eternity. As a result, I have spared myself from wasting time, money, and energy on things that have no eternal value.

Rewards

Something else we learn from that parable is that God rewards us. Just like any parent who delights in rewarding their children, God delights in rewarding His. What's so amazing about this is that God gives us the gifts, opportunities, and resources to use those gifts, then He blesses us in abundance when we use them! God would much rather bless us than have to correct us. "Remember that the Lord will reward each one of us for the good we do, whether we are slaves or free" (Ephesians 6:8, NLT). That should motivate us to make the most of every opportunity!

I have heard people say that we should not do things for a reward but that we should do them because it is simply the right thing to do. I have to ask those who reason like that if they expect a paycheck for their work at the end of the week. See my point? I don't have the space to list all the verses on God's character as a rewarder. Sometimes we need to be reminded of the promise of a reward, in order to endure the pain. Jesus promised a reward to every church He wrote to in Revelation. There is great promise and reward for maximizing what God gives us to advance the kingdom and bless others!

The Ultimate Choice

This entire book was birthed from a sermon I wrote. As I was writing the sermon, the Lord said to me, "This will be your magnum opus." This is a Latin phrase describing something like a grand piece of artwork, music, literature, or, in my case, the most important work of a writer. I did not set out to be a writer. At the time I thought God was just speaking in regard to my sermon. In fact, I never completed 10th grade English! I hated the subject, and during that time in my life I was not a reader. It wasn't until I had finished the sermon that I realized he was talking about turning it into a book, or as I have been calling it, a guide.

In late 2021 my wife and I began to pray and seek God about this book. We realized there was something about the year 2022. Because of all the holidays, we decided we would begin the project of writing the book in 2022. We knew the book would be about truth, and about the choices we make. I wanted to use the movie The Matrix as the main analogy, using the *red* and *blue* pills as examples of accepting or rejecting the truth. I had actually used The Matrix as the vehicle in the sermon, but since this was going to be published, I didn't want to violate any copyright laws, so I started looking for a different narrative.

Initially, I was very discouraged because I really wanted to use the stark contrast of red and blue to symbolize the choices we have to make. However, I felt like God had another plan, and He did. He used my encounter on the beach with the sea turtles! I did not see it coming, and they worked out so much better, going so much deeper. I was still able to incorporate the red and blue choices using the true red light, and the artificial blue lights, which we examined in choice two. Truly, when God tells us his plans, we laugh! His plans are always higher, and better than we can imagine!

In addition to God using the sea turtles to give me the inspiration for the book, there was something about 2022 (as I stated earlier), and the number 22 that I felt was significant. I have studied the Hebrew alphabet, and I know there are only 22 letters in their alphabet. The 22nd letter is the letter Tav, and it sounds like our letter "T". Tav means "truth," and truth is what this message is all about. We started seeing 22 in everything. We realized in 2022 we would have been together 22 years. In 2022 I celebrate 22 years of sobriety. Ironically, when we were thinking of the Matrix (originally), we looked up the year it was made — it had been 22 years. In fact, it was released on December 22! I also realized by looking in my journal that the day I first felt inspired to write this guide was on Nov. 22. I looked up the Hebrew number 1122, because I felt it meant something, and it did. The Hebrew number 1122 in Strong's concordance is the word *grammateus*, which means *to write*! We were seeing signs like this for weeks! We went to dinner one evening with some friends, and one couple unexpectedly brought their grandchild. Once they were seated, the waitress came out with something for the toddler to color on and gave him one crayon. We noticed the crayon was half *red* and half *blue*; my wife and I couldn't believe it! I took the crayon home with me and kept it as confirmation. Things like that just kept happening.

The thing that put a cap on the calling to write the book came when we were in Ohio at a conference. On the last day of the conference, a popular worship band was there performing, and the worship leader shared with the congregation how the Holy Spirit kept impressing on him 2022! I could not believe it! I knew it was another confirmation. I could not have put all those things together in a million years! Since the Matrix was off the table, I began to think of how to use the red and blue colors as choices. I had some idea because of the red light and the red letters of Jesus. It wasn't long after that – that the revelation of the blue lights came. However, I felt there was still a deeper truth to be revealed.

A few weeks had gone by when I received a phone call from a friend. We began talking about someone we knew who needed salvation. My friend started talking about the book 22 minutes in hell. I thought, there is the number 22 again! So, I did some research on Hell. Hell is described in the Bible as burning sulfur, we see that in Revelation 20. "The devil who deceived them was thrown into the lake of *fire* and *sulfur*, where the beast and the false prophet are also. They will be tormented day and night forever and ever" (Revelation 20:10, WEB). What I learned is that sulfur burns blue! The flames of hell are blue. I was sharing what I discovered with a co-worker who has over 16 years in prison ministry, and he told me about a man who had a life after death experience. The man went to Hell and said he was heading toward blue flames! However, the Lord saved him in that moment. He said he later learned that someone he knew had been praying for him at the time of his death, (thank God for that prayer warrior). I then resolved that I had the deeper meaning for the color blue.

Redeemed by the Blood

When my daughter was 22 years old (notice the number 22 again), she went into a bar and began drinking until she was completely intoxicated. As a result of her judgment being severely impaired, she attempted to drive home. Not only was that a bad decision, but it was also the middle of winter. While she was driving, she lost control of the vehicle and hit a telephone pole. She hit the pole so hard that the front bumper of the car wrapped around to the back bumper of the car. The impact knocked the transformer loose from the pole but did not hit her car. She miraculously survived the crash with only minor injuries!

A few days later, my wife and I had to go to the salvage yard where the car was taken to handle some paperwork. As we were pulling into the scrap yard, we saw the car. The moment we saw the car my wife burst into tears. I had never seen a car folded in two before! I walked around the car and peered into the driver side, I could see the air bag had deployed a there was some blood on the bag — not much, but there was enough there to speak volumes to me. I was reminded of what God had said to the Israelites when he was about release the destroying angel on the land. He said, "Put the lamb's blood on your door post.... The blood shall be to you for a token on the houses where you are. When I see the blood, I will pass over you, and no plague will be on you to destroy you when I strike the land of Egypt" (Exodus 12:13, WEB). All I could think about is how I'm in a covenant with God, and how God remembered the blood of the covenant and spared my child! Today, my daughter is married and has blessed my wife and me with three grandchildren and she is passionate about her relationship with the Lord!

The only way to escape eternal destruction is to be redeemed by the blood of Jesus — **the color red**. The other choice is to reject His free gift of grace and spend eternity in the burning sulfur of Hell — **the color blue**. See, I never needed my own analogy. As everything came together, I realized the Lord did not need my Matrix narrative or any other narrative. He has always offered his own version of choosing between **red** or **blue**. If you choose to follow the *red light of truth*, you will discover your destiny and find salvation; if you follow the *blue lights* of the Devil, your life will end in disillusionment and destruction.

My prayer, as we close, is that you will *choose red*, and that this guide will help you in making, and affirming that this is the best choice you could make for your life. As you follow God's best for you, His destiny for your life; I pray you find a life of abundance in Christ in this world, and in eternity with our Father. I pray that you follow the red light of the truth, just as our friends, the sea turtles, followed the red light to their destiny.

CHARTER GUIDE ELEVEN
"The Empty Shell"

Your eleventh and final choice is either to *believe God's word is the truth* or to *believe your own version of the truth.*

- What do you believe about eternal life?

- What do you believe about Heaven and Hell?

- Do you try to treat everyone like they were Jesus himself?

- What do you do to be faithful with what God has given you?

- How do you make day-to-day decisions with eternity in mind?

- How do you hope to be rewarded at the Judgment Seat?

THE ULTIMATE CHOICE

You have to choose to either *believe God's word is the truth* or *believe your own version of the truth.* *It's your choice.*

Scripture: Don't lay-up treasures for yourselves on the earth, where moth and rust consume, and where thieves break through and steal; but lay up for yourselves treasures in heaven, where neither moth nor rust consume, and where thieves don't break through and steal; for where your treasure is, there your heart will be also.
-Matthew 6:19-21, WEB

Thought: We will live forever; the end of our physical life is only the beginning of our eternal life. *Where* will we live forever is a choice. Eternity only gives us two options, Heaven or Hell, and we have to choose for ourselves which one.

NOTES:

As I was thinking about this last choice, these words came to my mind: Knowing the **truth** will keep you from being **misled**, but it will not keep you from being **misread,** because not everyone chooses to follow the **red light** to **destiny.**

"Awake, you who sleep, and arise from the dead, and Christ will shine on you."
                    -Ephesians 5:14, WEB

Printed in the United States
by Baker & Taylor Publisher Services